THESE THREE REMAIN:
FAITH, HOPE, AND LOVE

Don and Deborah Quattlebum

WESTBOW
PRESS
A DIVISION OF THOMAS NELSON

Scripture quotations taken from the New American Standard Bible®,
Copyright © 1960, 1962, 1963, 1968, 1971, 1972, 1973, 1975, 1977, 1995 by
The Lockman Foundation. Used by permission." (www.Lockman.org)

WestBow Press books may be ordered through booksellers or by contacting:

WestBow Press
A Division of Thomas Nelson
1663 Liberty Drive
Bloomington, IN 47403
www.westbowpress.com
1 (866) 928-1240

Because of the dynamic nature of the Internet, any web addresses or
links contained in this book may have changed since publication and
may no longer be valid. The views expressed in this work are solely those
of the author and do not necessarily reflect the views of the publisher,
and the publisher hereby disclaims any responsibility for them.

Any people depicted in stock imagery provided by Thinkstock are models,
and such images are being used for illustrative purposes only.
Certain stock imagery © Thinkstock.

ISBN: 978-1-4908-1429-2 (sc)
ISBN: 978-1-4908-1431-5 (hc)
ISBN: 978-1-4908-1430-8 (e)

Library of Congress Control Number: 2013919847

Printed in the United States of America.

WestBow Press rev. date: 11/05/2013

We dedicate this book:

> To Jesus, for loving us, for being our hope, and giving us faith;

> To our parents, for bringing us up with love, guiding us to hope, and encouraging our faith;

> To each other, for unwavering love, keeping the hope bright, and walking together in faith;

> To our sons, Donald and David, for keeping our faith active, for keeping us hopeful, and for sharing love with us;

> To our grandsons, Matthew and Maverick, for carrying on the faith, being full of hope, and being so easy to love.

We want to acknowledge the incredible love, support, and the many prayers by some awesome friends to us and the ministry. It would take another book to tell all the experiences we have had together:

>Pastors Louis and Irene Soros, Destiny Christian Life Center, Citrus Heights, California

>Pastors Jeff and Tammy Bills, The Dwelling Place, Woodland, California

>Rev. Linda Cady, Associate Minister, The King's Domain, Inc.

>Rev. Tammy Hartman, Assistant Minister, The King's Domain, Inc.

>Calvin and Renae Lamb, Lead Worshipers, Destiny Christian Life Center

We want to give a Special Thanks to everyone that worked with us at Westbow Press, a division of Thomas Nelson, for their patience and help.

CONTENTS

THERE ARE THREE THAT REMAIN

We are important to God. He holds us close to His heart. His thoughts and focus are always on us. He loves us unconditionally, deeply, and passionately. There is nothing we can do that will make Him love us less. And there is nothing that we can do that will make Him love us more. He loves us with all that He is and has proven and shown the depth of His love through His manifestation in Jesus Christ.

He has always thought more of us than we think of ourselves. He wants us to know the feelings for us He holds in His heart and His willingness to bless us and to show us favor. He wants us to see ourselves as He sees us. We are His, and He is ready to show us how important we are to Him. A greater understanding and a greater experience of our relationships with Him await us. We will come to know Him in the way He wants us to know Him—through His restoration of all things to His original plan.

The times have come full circle, to where we now have the opportunity once again to walk and talk openly with Him. Our relationships with Him are restored. If we would just believe and receive, all things would be done in us and through us to restore all things. He is looking to manifest Himself in incredible ways in us and for our sakes.

There was an incredible price paid for us to have the relationship with God for which He created us. He wants to be with us more than we want to be with Him. We can have a better understanding of the importance He places upon us if we would have the faith, hope, and love active in us in the way He wants. Through these three spiritual qualities, we would have the view of ourselves that God intends.

Through Him, we rise to the place where we know who we are in Him and obtain the life of the Kingdom of God. Through Jesus, God is restoring all things to His original plan— an unbroken fellowship and relationship with Him. We need to see ourselves through the payment made by the events of Jesus' life.

It isn't about what we haven't done; it is about what He has done for us (Romans 8:28). The work that He has done will wend its way throughout our lives. Our relationships with God are more than spiritual events. Our relationships take in all that we are, all that we can be, and all that we will be. Because of our faith in Him, we will develop a higher capacity for appreciating Him.

Through the active workings of our faith, hope, and love, we attain the measure that God created in us (Ephesians 4:12–13). For too long, we have looked through the evil and darkness that entered this world in the beginning and have not seen the fullness of His promise.

We need to adjust our sight.

There are times we may find that our views of our lives may need adjusting. We may need to reexamine or take inventory of what is at work in our lives. This examination can reveal those things that we may have lost, those things that have been damaged and are in need of repair, and those things that remain in a strong position for us to stand.

We may even find the Holy Spirit working on our behalf when we didn't know that He was there. The loss of anything or the damaging of things we hold dear can be devastating to us if we allow them to be, especially when we do not recognize what we really have built up in our lives.

We may not see things in their correct positions or in the right light. We sometimes lack an understanding of who we really are and the work that Jesus accomplished on the cross, in the grave, through His ascension, at Pentecost, and by pouring out the Holy Spirit on every believer. We need to draw closer to Him and to come to a new understanding of who God is, what He has accomplished, and the influence He desires to have in our lives (Ephesians 3:11–19). All that we are and who we are rests in Him and the influence of faith, hope, and love.

Our relationships will become stable as we draw closer to Him and as we understand all that He is to us.

The life of humanity can be understood in three general stages: first, at creation; second, under rebellion (a time of destruction); and third, with Christ (our re-creation). One could go into greater detail exploring these stages, but consider, for now, some basic and general observations of what I am trying to illustrate. There is much we may yet discover in the lessons of creation, destruction, and re-creation.

The flow of history shows how humanity has reacted and lived in these stages. The records contained within the Bible give us many accounts of failure and success of different people living through particular stages. Recorded histories outside of the biblical records are just as important for seeing our reactions to our foundations. Now we live with a different viewpoint. Humanity has gone through the first two stages and is now—as a whole—in the third.

The first stage gives us our beginnings and shows how we had a free and close relationship with God. At the time of creation, we walked with Him and talked face-to-face with Him. This is why He created us: to be with Him and to enjoy that relationship. We were made to bring pleasure to Him. The life that humanity lived in the beginning shows us how God favored us and shared His authority with us.

In the beginning, all things were as He purposed. We were free, healthy, and strong with Him. We lived in His Spirit and walked with Him. God's Word was believed and lived out. There was no doubt or rebellion. We lived in strength of the faith, hope, and love for which we were created.

We participated with Him in caring for His creation.

There was no darkness of sin and nothing to hinder us from being with Him. We reaped all the benefits of the relationship we had with Him. We walked with no fear but in the confidence of what God had given us. All things were as they were supposed to be and how they will be again someday. We were full of faith, hope, and love. Nothing was hidden from us as we had time with God. This stage was perfect, until an evil and darkness crawled into the midst of things and deposited its deceit and foul waste. This started the next stage of humanity.

In the second stage, everything took a turn that was not in our best interest. In this stage, an evil entered the scene and changed everything. Once this evil entered life, all things were dragged down into heaviness and a trap of darkness. We could no longer see who we were, and we became lost from all that was ours. We hid ourselves from the answer to our problems, further sealing our fates to be running forever, unless someone stepped in to intervene.

We gave up on the faith, hope, and love that were the major parts of the foundation underlying all things. The evil would not have won if we had stood in the open. We were deceived, and we lost out in the open relationship we had with the Light of our lives. Humanity was no longer free. Rebellion, sin, and darkness became the rule instead of the faith, hope, and love that God had planned.

Humanity lost much in this stage. Something had to be done. We would not have lasted if things had kept going as they were. Humanity was on the road to complete destruction. The evil was powerful, but the evil would find its defeat in the third stage of humanity, because of the power of God in faith, hope, and love. God was going to reveal Himself through Jesus (Romans 16:24–27; Ephesians 1:18–23). It was time that we entered the third stage, so that all things would be restored to the condition God had intended for them at the beginning.

God had never abandoned His original plan for us. He never stopped working toward the time when all things would be according to His heart.

The third stage began with the greatest of events to be seen and experienced since creation. God chose at this point in our history to break into the flow of time and reveal His love in the flesh. He came Himself into our space because He loved us so much. God had nothing to prove but everything to correct and restore. He came to break the hold that evil and darkness had over us. Through the events of the life of Jesus, we were shown a new way of living (Hebrews 10:19–22).

So much had transpired that we had to be re-taught what it meant to have faith, hope, and love. He wasn't proving who He was; He was restoring our memory of who He always is.

In His life and through His sacrifice, everything was set straight so that we might once again have a free relationship with God. Through the events from the cross to the coming of the Holy Spirit, God re-created us and restored His image in us (2 Corinthians 5:17). We can once again have face-to-face fellowship and conversation with God. He did this for us, and now we must decide to believe or reject His gifts of love and salvation.

Through faith, hope, and love, we can stand in the promises of God and know Him as He wants to be known.

We are on a strong foundation in our relationships with Him when we believe in Him. This is the point of history we find ourselves in now. We must decide to believe or reject what God is opening for us. There are those who have become accustomed to the dark and the loss of fellowship. It is difficult for some to believe that things can be better. When it has been a long time since one has had faith or experienced hope or even known love, there isn't always a quick jump to receive truth.

When the foundation of our lives has been shaken, we need to return to that foundation and restore it with the faith, hope and love that remain with us in all situations and circumstances. We are built and created on the basis of who and what Jesus did (1 Corinthians 3:11), not on someone else's feelings or offenses. We will make a decision to shore up our foundations or neglect them further.

The foundational stones of our lives and of who we are can be damaged, in disrepair, and hidden if we do not maintain our life view and disciplines. The Chief Cornerstone will always remain the same and untouched for any Believer. This is the same for the world, but it has rejected His importance. The cornerstone is and always will be Jesus Christ (Ephesians 3:20). In His image, by His power given through Him as the Word of God, we were created and established in our faith (Colossians 2:7, 2 Peter 1:12). In Christ is all we are and are to be.

We are defined and measured by who Jesus is in our lives.

We must not let the truth be ignored that is in us by His Word and Spirit. This truth is in and established in us (1 John 1:2). This truth is a power that will raise us to the place of His greatest manifestation (John 8:32; 1 John 4:4). The evil tried to rewrite truth, but it was no longer the truth. Jesus cannot be changed (Hebrews 13:8). Jesus is never damaged or lost, but our ability was changed by sin and the rebellion against God and His ways.

Jesus can and will restore His truth for everyone.

When we believe in Him we can then live in the sure foundation of faith, hope, and love.

Anyone would feel better about himself, about his life, and all he may be going through when he has some stability. Everyone likes to know what they can count on. Most people like to know that they can stand on their own and that what they stand on is firm. To start anything from a rocky and shaky position does not yield success. It is not that success is impossible with such a start but that the odds are against it and that such a start makes a good ending difficult.

When we start with Jesus, we will end with Jesus, and there is no failure in Him (Hebrews 10:23). We need to know whom we believe.

In our examination of ourselves, it would be beneficial to find ways to build up the faith and truth of God in our lives. This is where faith, hope, and love come to our attention and into our focus. We understand that Jesus is eternal (1 Timothy 1:17; Hebrews 7:24–25). We also know that His Word will stand forever (1 Peter 1:25). We cannot build on any foundation than that which is centered on the person and reality of Jesus (1 Corinthians 3:11). We need eternal things active in our lives in order for us to build on that which God has already placed in us.

We have to build with eternal things in order for us to stand in all that life may bring. The flesh cannot build into the Spirit, but the Spirit can build into and influence the flesh toward eternal and spiritual things. When we realize that the flesh is weak, we can also realize that it can be strengthened by the Holy Spirit. Being weak is not saying that we will be defeated. When our lives are based on faith, hope, and love, we are raised to a new capacity and strength of all the inheritance we have in Him (Ephesians 1:9-12).

The flesh, things of this world, or things that are temporal cannot take the weight of the Spirit or of those things that are eternal. In fact, things of the flesh or of the world are in battle with those things of the Spirit (2 Corinthians 10:3–4). We must build into our self the capacity for the things that are of God. These things are those things of the Holy Spirit.

We do this through faith, hope, and love. These three that remain give us access to all that we need that "pertains to life and godliness" (2 Peter 1:3 NASB). It is a thing of the Spirit that leads us further into the things of the Spirit. A perfection comes to all things as we "put on love" (Colossians 3:14 NASB). We need to come into an agreement and into alignment with the things the Spirit brings into our lives to enhance and deepen our relationships with Him.

Since the days when evil and darkness entered into the works of humanity, we have had difficulty yielding to anything else but the evil. Though we now live in a time when all that has been defeated, many are still working on getting the bend out of them so that they can come into alignment. This is where faith, hope, and love help to focus us on Jesus, who has paid the price and leads us through the Kingdom establishment by the Holy Spirit.

These three—faith, hope, and love—are the constant for our lives in the Spirit.

These are what bring our flesh into alignment and subjection to the Holy Spirit. The battle of the flesh cannot be fought and won by things of the flesh. We must put on and use the full armor that God provides for us (Ephesians 6:10–18). These three give us the place to stand, for when we have "done everything we can to stand, keep standing" (Ephesians 6:13–14, author's paraphrase). Faith, hope, and love are strong.

These three meet our expectations and are ever present to help us in all we do. We can endure because of their presence in our lives. There is nothing too hard for us to experience. They will dwell in us to make us more like Him. We know this because of the promises of God, and His Word lasts forever. Many are in the process of reprioritizing so that these three remain and dwell in us. They do so by the Holy Spirit, and they each become significant for our continued benefit in Jesus and His Kingdom.

Each of these is important to our lives. They are important individually but stronger as a whole. These three that remain are working in us to mature and grow us into the fullness of who we are to be (Ephesians 4:14–19). As we allow the faith, hope, and love to have their way and a place in our lives, more of the image of God will be revealed in us.

We were created in His image, and it was hidden when the evil and darkness came. It is time for the entire image be seen and that God manifest Himself in His fullness in and through our lives. Each of these three has a major role in making this happen in each of our lives.

It becomes important to know these three, what they are, and how we interact with them. We want to look at these three as the following: faith, the God-possible; hope, the God-perspective; love, the God-power. In faith, we participate with the Holy Spirit to see all things come to being through Him. Through the activity of our faith, we overcome all things that may try to stand against what God is doing. In faith, we know there is nothing impossible for Him.

With hope, we see the Father and can follow Him closer, to know Him as He wants to be known. Much is lost because we are not seeing things in the perspective that God sees them. Hope becomes about seeing what God sees and how He sees us. It isn't about getting our way but about staying the "way" that God is showing and leading us. As we follow Him, our hope grows, helping us to avoid the traps that the evil and darkness may have left behind in their defeat.

By love, we are able to go beyond ourself and bring together all things for the pleasure of the Father. The word *love* is used a lot, but many do not activate the actual power and strength of love. Love is more than a great feeling. It is more than a kind act. Love is the greatest of these three and needs to be held dear in our lives. God is love, and we must allow that image to be seen through us.

In the pursuit of God, we need these three—faith, hope, and love—to be active and strong in our lives. It isn't about showing others how far we have come but how these three have never failed. There are three that remain in order for us to bring the most glory, honor, and worship to God, our Father. We have been built upon a strong foundation of Jesus, and it is seen because these three remain and dwell in us.

Faith, hope, and love will bring us into the Kingdom of God lifestyle, where we are like Him and not compromised in any way.

FAITH: THE GOD-POSSIBLE

The Pursuit of Faith

Whether you want to call it a religious resurgence, spiritual awakening, or even a revival; something is happening to cause many to question not only the idea of God but their individual concept of faith. Their search goes beyond looking for the meaning and/or purpose of life. People are searching for a viable and powerful spiritual reality that many churches and religious groups have left behind, but the search continues for a faith that satisfies.

The "common church" of nearly all denominational or nondenominational persuasion is in crisis over faith. Many of these common churches have defined themselves and their doctrinal stances as the "faith," but people see the empty hold that it can have on one's life. The common-church faith is a guideline for membership into what would be better described as a social club than a kingdom.

Faith has been reduced to a rule or guideline, rather than a power or a necessary element in our relationships with God. We have been asked to work for a place in the Kingdom rather than have faith for it. We are told to know a statement of fact or knowledge, rather than walk in the Spirit, activating our faith to show who we know. We are asked to build our relationships in the common church, rather than with God.

Here is a nearly forgotten fact: we were created by God with the capacity and ability to "live by faith." Everything we need, we have been given by Him. Everything we need for life and godliness is provided by Him (2 Peter 1: 2–4). Being the good God that He is; He has made the way for us to enjoy all He has created.

In the first week of creation, God announced, "It is good!" He announced His pleasure in all that was around Him. God's pleasure is at stake. It is not just our souls or salvation at stake but all that He has envisioned for us to experience. He wants us to experience His love and pleasure. Faith is important to that. Faith is necessary in order to please God (Hebrews 11:6). Faith will open our lives to experience all that He is.

All is made possible by God when we allow ourselves to live by and operate in life by Faith. This is the great revelation of the Reformation—wholeness by faith. When you read of the "heroes of faith," as given to us in Hebrews 11, you see that their faith was God-pleasing, powerful, and life changing. It does not affect us just individually; it affects all those with whom we have a relationship.

In many of the accounts and stories of the life of Jesus, we see incredible acts of faith revealing divine power. His teaching has encouragements and standards in order to live the His-Kingdom lifestyle. Everything about Him is to awaken our faith in Him and to live it out every day. It should be no surprise that faith is a central theme in believing and following Jesus.

'Seeing a lone fig tree by the road,
He came to it and found nothing
on it except leaves only.'
(Matthew 21:19, NASB)

Now, you may ask, "What does this have to do with faith?" It actually has a lot to do with faith. In the current age of our belief in Jesus; I would guess that most people's faith has been limited to salvation. Yet there is more to our faith than what we have been commonly taught and even more to its meaning.

None of this is to say that there is anything wrong with having faith only for salvation. This is but the beginning of an incredible journey and relationship that we have with Jesus. It is incomplete and is not whole; it does not complete the works of our faith. The Holy Spirit does all things to completion and wholeness because of the work activated in us by faith. Jesus declared on the cross, "It is finished!" (John 19:20 NASB). Now in faith we will see the full meaning of this declaration.

It seems that more individuals have chosen to work for their salvation and have called it faith for salvation. They do all that they can for security but feel more insecure as they go along, not fully comprehending the capacity of their faith and the depth of His love.

We cannot work for our wholeness; we must have faith for it. And if we are whole, then there is an incredible kingdom life opened to us that most have yet to experience—most have not even thought or imagined it. A broken vessel does not have the capacity to be full, though it can have wholeness again. It does have the potential for it and more.

The absence of a snack becomes a lesson of faith and a show of power. Jesus chooses to release a key principle of the Kingdom of Heaven under surprising circumstances. With just a word spoken in faith, any and all circumstances and perceptions change. He could not find a fig, so no one would ever find one on this tree.

In this, He chose to make an object lesson of the tree. With a word, He cursed the tree and amazed everyone around by what he could do and by what happened. He was revealing more and more of His nature and purposes through an act of faith and power. As there is more to what we call salvation; there is more to faith.

Many do not think about God in terms of His needs or His desires. The concept that God would be lonely, hurt, or even hungry seems foreign to our belief of God. So we have a tendency to miss things in the life of Christ or to deny the very basics of our belief system. The idea that He is all God and all man at the same time can prove difficult to comprehend.

Jesus is God in the flesh, so it would seem reasonable that what we see in one is a reflection or mirror image of the other. They are one; there is no separation in the two. We do not serve more than one God. Our perceptions have to change to account for the concept of God being free of time and space. In this one instance, we see in both realms of reality—His and ours.

God shattered the barrier of our "time and space" in order for His plan to be completed. Through man, the barrier was allowed to be set up; this barrier separated man from God. Within the barrier, sickness and sin began to incubate and to destroy the faith given to us. This was what caused Him to reinsert Himself and breathe faith again into our dying souls.

Mankind has become blinded by the weight of sin and the bent vision it had caused. Mankind needs to be lifted by the weight of His glory. Once the sin is washed away, we can fly to the heights of heaven. We are to be washed by the price of His blood in order to be bathed in the light of His glory. There is no blindness in the kingdom, but the light of the kingdom blinds those things and powers found in the darkness.

God became a man, shattering the barrier, so that we could observe and experience the life that was intended for us. He gave to us a tangible opportunity to experience the relationship with Him that He always intended. As faith came alive in us, so did our fellowship with God. We were once again able to walk through the garden of creation and to talk with Him openly.

Our eyes must remain open to see the kingdom possibilities for us and those around us. Our minds have to think in paths not traveled by many. God became flesh in order to communicate truths of His kingdom. We must hear and see the entire message, not just the parts we are comfortable with or that we like, but all that God gives voice to for our lives and righteousness.

The traditions of science and of the common church limit the thinking of most people. When we have been trained in one path of thinking and/or living, it is hard to break from that pattern. It is easier to miss important paths and revelations. Being so-called "open-minded" doesn't mean a person will pursue thoughts beyond himself. To overcome the prejudices and limited thinking, we will find a need to transform our minds (Romans 12:1–2). We can no longer allow the evil and darkness to rule our thinking, but we will find surrender to the Holy Spirit the best and only way to freedom.

This will require a retraining of our thinking—a revisioning of the path of knowledge. Biblically, our minds must be renewed to think in the path and levels of God (Romans 12:1–3). Our thinking cannot be bound by the flesh or by any circumstance. There is a level of thinking and knowing that is Holy Spirit and faith inspired.

Through ourselves, we see the impossible; through the level of faith, we see the God-possible. This is not just positive thinking, any deep secret, or hidden law of life. God, from the beginning, created in us a great potential that was squandered away for a piece of fruit. Since that time, man has always struggled with the immediate rather than ruling the moment.

In this void, we have forgotten that we can satisfy the immediate need without violating any standard of faith. We need to think with "kingdom thinking" and see with "kingdom sight"—thinking and seeing which is outside of ourselves. Faith once again brings creation fellowship into reality.

God's thoughts were on us during the act of creation. This is how God came to us—outside from His realm into ours. We must rise to His realm, the King's domain. We are given an incredible opportunity to experience God in the way He intended, just as Adam did in the beginning.

After the "fall of man" from faith to bondage, man operated under fear. This fear came from a pattern of thinking that was negative, manipulative, and absent of truth. Man forgot his image was based and patterned after God.

The proper way of thinking was to think as God. The people listed in Hebrews 11 are highlighted not because of specific acts but because of the renewal of their faith. They showed how once again man could walk with God and have face-to-face fellowship with the Father.

It is time to live by faith. This will call for a renewal of our souls. And in order to renew our faith, we will need to renew our minds (Romans 12:1–3). In order to renew our minds, there will need to be a new and re-breathing of God's Holy Spirit into us.

Some would call this revival, but it is the ultimate act and activation of faith—the same we started with and need to keep going with. It is time to take His hand and never let Him go, a true exercise of our faith in Him. Trusting and listening only to Him is the only way to live the kingdom lifestyle. It is truly the way of faith that we have been called to live and to enjoy.

This act of faith restores our wholeness. We are back in a position of being able to walk and talk with God, face-to-face. As it was in the beginning, so it is to be now. This is not the end but the continuation of the plan of God, written in times before writing.

We must learn to live in Him. Our focus, then, becomes Him and not us. We were made in His image and were to be like Him, but we were bent by sin. Now that we have by faith been straightened again, it is His image that we are conformed and must learn to reflect Him in all that we do and think.

Our needs and God's pleasure blends through our faith to fulfill the plan of salvation written long before the fall. The plan is that you and I will walk with God, face-to-face and side by side. We will romance God and be romanced by Him. It is a pure relationship that was lost for so long which is now regenerated with a rising of our faith. Our search is nearly over as we return to the beginning of all things. By faith, all things are restored to the original plan of God.

God is the all-sufficient One, so why would He have any need? It is because of our great need to live above our current level and rise above the mundane by seeing that there is more to this life if we would but have faith. We have always been at the center of God's heart. We are surrounded by His love, and He hides us in His heart of love. Our active faith, when in touch with His heart, brings the openness and fruitfulness He created in the beginning and the image that was created in us will be revealed and manifested again as we live and have faith.

He has a need to see us live to our potential. He has a need to have and find pleasure in us. We were created for Him. There was purpose in that creation, and though that power of that purpose was bartered away, through faith it is ours again. We no longer need to work at who we are but rest in Him and know who we are.

In His need, He chose to pay the price and to show us the way to live as He purposed for us. He bought back our freedom of faith. This goes beyond any freedom of choice or will; faith is the sight to our relationships in God. In following Him and rising to the power of faith, we can hear and act as and for Him. Our beings are made whole.

His need is not based on anything that is necessary to His life. His need is based upon who He is. It is His state of being that we are to reflect. His need is not for what He can get but what He can give. He has already given Himself in death; now He offers Himself in life. He offers life in a more abundant way (John 10:10b).

An act of faith gives to us this life, and it is an eternal life.

His command is simple yet full of power:

"Have faith!"

This is a simple command from our Creator. Coming from someone who exists above time and space, He is eternal and without measurement or containment. By faith we will stand with Him daily.

Though many have accepted a limit to the physical life, there is no limit to faith and what we can reap from faith sowed into our lives. The entire life of Jesus was about the journey and adventure into the better life of the kingdom. Jesus did the work, set the path, paid the price, and gave us the means to enter into this better life.

It is all by *faith*.

He promotes and encourages us to not only examine our faith but to exercise our faith in all aspects of our lives. That faith is not given the limits that so many have placed upon it. Others have limited their lives and faith to what they know—time and space. God leads us beyond the limits and shows us how to inject ourselves into and through the limits. This is time to remove the walls, not just go outside of them.

The incredible dimensions of God's love become more apparent to us as we hunger for Him. He loves us unconditionally, deeply and passionately. He can't love us any more than He did and does. There is nothing that we can do to make Him love us more, and there is nothing we can do to make Him Love us less.

Love is who He is, and it is all of what He is. Love makes up His entire being. We need to know it in all of its dimensions—the heights, widths, and depths (Ephesians 3:18–19). He wants us to live this life of faith not only to our benefit but to His heart's desire of pure fellowship with us. He has missed us.

His need for creation to be set right drove His heart to sacrifice Himself for us. There is no way He could show His love any greater. It is all for us in a simple act of faith. Believe, and have eternal life and wholeness.

We need to see Him for who and what He is. Our faith gives us that sense of being that allows us to hear and see Him for the truth of who He is. His love and the faith He gave us solves all the mysteries we could ever imagine. All things will open up to us through faith. By faith, we see Him and His kingdom. There is nothing hidden from us because of His love and the faith that He freely gave us.

Whether it was a miracle, parable, or any other act of love, it was all for our benefit, to help us walk this walk of faith. It was more than a new feeling; it was an activation and restoration of an experience long forgotten by man—a face-to-face relationship with God. Faith can renew that relationship and experience—in us and in others.

We are not ruled by circumstances, but we rule our circumstances by the faith we are given. Faith brings us back to the original creation within the Kingdom of God. Jesus restored the ways of the kingdom. Creation was restored to its original purposes and plans.

The foundations of the world were pulled back together. Repairs were done where needed. There was a restoration of those things that had been neglected; and in those spots that were missing, the foundation was laid again for life and godliness. The foundation was no longer words and laws but a relationship. The foundation is now you and I, with Jesus as the cornerstone. We make up the building (Ephesians 2:19–22).

It is time that the Kingdom of God be revealed and be established for everyone to see and experience. Jesus took every opportunity to expose the Kingdom of Heaven. He laid out the entire plan through His miracles, parables, and all acts of faith and love. Through the faith He gave us, we can follow these plans and be a part of the revelation of the love and power of God, as our worship and witness of who He is in our lives.

Heaven and earth have crossed the lines of each reality. There were no walls to overcome due to the fact there are no longer walls. Jesus said, "You too will recognize the closeness of the kingdom when you see these things taking place" (Luke 21:31, author's paraphrase). You have this capability in you—*have faith.*

You are a part of the Kingdom of God.

It is of no matter that some did not grasp the meanings of these things. He allowed His life and His faith to bring to man the experience of the presence of God and His kingdom that was to be theirs from the beginning. It was our privilege and right as believers and as a part of the kingdom. At first, we gave away so much for so little, without much thought of what it all meant.

Through the life and actions of Jesus, mankind was once again given a faith opportunity by choosing the Kingdom of

God, rather than a kingdom of ourselves. We were allowed to see what it meant to rule and have dominion. What God had freely given at creation was freely given with re-creation.

Our belief is not about our understanding of these things, but it is about our obedience to Him. Things are not lost out of our ignorance but out of our disobedience. Faith and obedience are related and dependent on one another. In order for us to not just prove our faith but to exercise it, we must be willing and ready to be obedient to what the Father shows and commands of us.

Adam's early failure blocked faith for all of mankind and transacted the sale of his soul rights to the enemy of God. All that was given to man now belonged to another who was not in line with the purposes of God. In fact, he stood in opposition to what the Father had purposed.

The enemy gained the keys to the kingdom through an act of deception and man's disobedience. The plan of the enemy was to do all that could be possibly done to destroy God's purposes. By entrapping man's ability to use his faith, the enemy was able to blind man from seeing the full purposes of God. This is a blindness that darkens all revelation, which is revealed in the light of the kingdom into which we are called.

Deception is a powerful weapon; by its very definition, it is a weapon of stealth. Many will be surprised by how easily they have been robbed of the capacity of faith to go beyond themselves, to once again be face-to-face with God. Many think it is about personal gain or going to church; they miss the point about this being about a relationship with Him.

It was not until Jesus came that our faith had a possibility of returning to the original plan. His lessons and declaration to "have faith" brought back man's sight to see the path to walk in faith. The psalmist, in 119:105 (author's paraphrase), says the "Word is the light showing the walkway." And John declared that Jesus was the Word. So He is the way (John 14:6) and the one who shows the way.

Jesus' death, burial, and resurrection purchased back our set of the keys of the kingdom. Now you and I, through faith, can return to the life we were destined to enjoy. The faith given to us presents us the opportunity to see the now and the possible futures.

All things are revealed in Him as we draw closer to Him. Our faith illumines the way and enlightens all those who exercise faith. Using or living to faith's potential is not for us but for Him.

The kingdom of this world, since man's failure, has been under the authority of more than someone evil; it has been evil itself, and it has had its way long enough. The price was paid for the title and keys of the kingdom to be transferred back to its rightful owners.

Our faith brings to light the reality of the price that Jesus paid to make this transfer. There was no partial payment; the entire bill was settled. There is no more for anyone to do or to pay to settle the cost of sin. We are free to pursue the life of faith that is intended to be lived and experienced.

We can finally live in the Kingdom of God as intended. So God came and shared faith by an act of love through His ultimate sacrifice. God planned for all the contingencies; He knew the weaknesses of man. God knew He would have to step in and impart faith to man, just as He breathed into man to make him a living being, a soul.

There no longer will be a reign of darkness to steal from us all that is rightfully ours. During the reign of destruction. A wall was built around our souls that needed to be torn down. But the kingdom of Light was about to build itself into the heart and life of any person who would believe. A great tree of healing and life would be established in our hearts.

The "Eden-type" life was now to be restored and the walls to be torn down. Freedom was to be had once again. The Tree of Life would now be freely shared, and the Tree of Knowledge would take root in each who would believe. We would be planted amid the river that flows all around us (Psalm 1). All kingdoms need water to last, and the Holy Spirit is the giver of unlimited living. The Holy Spirit is the water of creation and life.

In the beginning, the image of God was revealed in us through creation. There will be a re-creation in order for that image to be recognized in each of us (1 John 3:2). A revival would awaken the dead and reveal God in all of us. We will see the kingdom established for all to enjoy.

Believers will have to learn how to live; after knowing the bondage of death for so long. At last, we will live the promise of a life of wholeness (John 10:10)—no more sickness, no more pain; new life and full of joy.

There will have to be a new mind-set, a new way of thinking. This is more than a paradigm shift. It is a complete reformation of seeing, thinking, and living—a new revival of faith to change not only our thinking but our communities. In revival, a call for real repentance—not just a declaration of sorrow over sin but a change of our mind-sets and thoughts—will be heard.

Through Christ we were given back our ability to see God. We would again walk and talk, face-to-face with our heavenly Father, our King. Faith is given in order that all who would use this new faith could participate equally. We are on equal ground (Galatians 3:28), based upon our faith, not on anything about us. The incredible price that was paid by Jesus makes this all possible.

Faith, not law, was to be the rule.

This may seem contradictory, exchanging law for rule. This is no semantics game. Law has a tendency to restrict and limit production. We live in great freedom because of our active faith—the rule of faith.

The rule of faith has no limits; it is based on the limitless being of God.

The law is based on what we are able to do. Faith is based upon what God has done. As important as we are to the heart of God, He is more important to our faith and lives.

It was by faith that we were always to live (Habakkuk 2:4). Faith would cause many to experience the grace and mercy of their rightful King. Faith opens the door for an open relationship with Him. Jesus started by the establishing of His kingdom in the first twelve of His disciples.

Jesus was restoring the first things of creation. He brought us back to wholeness and our rightful place before God. The life of faith is a life of freedom, and knowing the truth sets us free

(John 8:32). To live by faith is both an Old and New Testament principle (Habakkuk 2:4; Romans 1:17). Jesus not only bridged the gap between the Testaments but made life as it was before the Testaments.

Due to the loss of faith and our privilege to be with God, we were no longer whole. Our lives were destined to search for our individual completeness with God. Jesus came to give back the faith and privilege we had each lost, in turn restoring our wholeness. He wants His original intention for creation to be restored.

He offers to you and me the opportunity to become complete and to meet face-to-face and walk hand in hand with Him again. There would no longer be incompleteness with the soul, but an overflow of love would indwell every citizen of this kingdom. The King would once again walk with man and have fellowship on a regular basis, but there was much to be taught, for much was forgotten. Our King wants us to trust Him and the responsibility that He takes for us.

Old habits do die hard and will take an exercise of faith to rewrite those habits. Man had forgotten how to walk worthily and in the authority that was given away by his failure at the beginning. Man lost his faith; he no longer believed as he should. Our bodies have been so conditioned to slavery that we have to transform our thinking for freedom. We have to learn to think as He does, rather than the selfish ways of man.

The capability of faith was to be activated in those who had relationship with the King. Each believer can walk, stand, and sit in the presence of their King and heavenly Father. We would once again be side by side, able to name, take care of, and bring all things under kingdom dominion. By faith, we will avoid the failure of the past and live as we should and can.

In Matthew 21:18–22; we see Jesus taking the opportunity to teach His disciples the principles of the Kingdom of God. Jesus, as King of this kingdom, knew the importance of declaring the ways, practices, and expectations of the kingdom that we are all to live in and enjoy. Jesus saw firsthand the devastation of sin; now, he looked for the restoration by faith. It was more than a demonstration of power; it was a demonstration of the power and control that faith could have.

Once again there will be an open relationship between God and His creation; King and subject. The kingdom returns its glory on earth. It is only by faith that we can fully appreciate all that we were offered. Jesus wasn't just saying, "Have faith!" He was commanding us to take hold of the faith He offered and to allow His faith to grip us.

This was one of many acts of power and faith that our King gave us as an example of kingdom life. The principles of power are activated by faith every day and in many ways. By faith, we no longer see through a darkened glass; we now have an open relationship with life and knowledge. We now can fellowship face-to-face, faith to faith, and glory to glory with our King, our God, and our heavenly Father.

Everything is to be as He originally created us. God wanted man to experience His love not just in the one-time acknowledgement of the death, burial, and resurrection of Jesus but in the everyday life as a child of the Kingdom. He is here to establish His kingdom in us, so that it will be over all the earth.

First things of creation are being restored to us and creation is being made new. God, in the beginning, began by breathing into us and making us a living soul. He has breathed upon us and has resurrected us to our place beside Him in acknowledgement of our faith. We will know Him as He wants to be known (Philippians 3:10).

Faith has cleared the way for us to breathe in the essence of the Holy Spirit; we are free to enjoy Him in wholeness. We will no longer have any reason to hide or cover ourselves, as Adam and Eve did. We are free to be as we were created to be, no longer ashamed or fearful of being exposed.

He is here to expose what God's plan and desire is for everyone. His great love opens the kingdom for all who would believe. We now enter into His through His love, which has paved the way by His grace and mercy. His love has restored our faith and given us hope. We no longer stand alone or entrapped, but we are surrounded by Him and have been made free.

His one act upon the cross and in the tomb is for an eternity of experiencing the presence of God. Our only act is to exercise the faith He has given us and in showing us how to live. These acts combine to be the greatest exercise of faith we can ever see or experience.

In Matthew 21, as in many other Scripture verses, we see that Jesus took the time to teach those around Him what it would take to be able to perform miracles, signs, and wonders; to actually affect and influence the world around them for the better. He showed what it was and will be like to have open fellowship again with the Father. The kingdom would be established in all of us.

He wants us to know the extent of our faith and what kingdom life has to offer.

As God told man in the beginning, we are now shown how to bring all things under authority and dominion. Jesus, in this one act, showed us how and what could happen when we know who we are and exercise our God-imparted authority. Unlike popular thought, we can and should affect people and circumstances around us. Our faith is for more than salvation but for living life as a whole person.

Jesus wasn't acting as God (Philippians 2:5–8). He set aside that possibility. He was standing as we all can—as children of God. Because of His trust and knowledge of the Father, by His faith He knew what He could do and how He was to lead the way. That same faith is imparted to us. Through the faith that He imparted to us, we can follow in His steps and fulfill the plan He originally laid out for us. We can know Him in a real way that only requires us to believe, and that is not a blind step of faith.

Everything that Jesus did was for our benefit. Whether we learn these lessons after all these years is also an act and intent of faith. We can be more than we appear, and we can live His life as He showed us and how He encouraged us to do. This is not an impossibility, for we can do everything necessary for "life and godliness" through Christ (Philippians 4:13; 2 Peter 1:2–4 NASB).

He wanted us to see that we can rule our surroundings and circumstances and not be ruled by them. Through our wholeness, our faith can make the difference. A simple exercise of our faith puts kingdom principles of life and righteousness to the forefront of our thinking. Restoration of the Kingdom was to include every aspect of our lives and beings.

We can influence in many ways the things and people around us. As we do the things that Jesus taught us and told us to do, we will make a difference in the community in which we live. There is purpose and drive behind all we hear of Him. He wants this to happen for us more than we want it to happen for His glory and pleasure.

Life took a turn that was not of His doing, and God will make things right again. Man followed the ways of the flesh and Satan long enough; it was time for the Kingdom to burst onto the scene of humanity and restore all things to their intended purposes. God wants to have open fellowship with His loved ones, so He chose a death in the flesh.

Man has shown himself unable to put himself back into his rightful position. It was only by an incredible act of sacrifice that God Himself would be able to put things right. There was now a way, through faith, to live our lives as it was originally intended. God restored creation to its original beauty and purposes.

This story in Matthew 21 isn't about a fruitless tree. The story is about living life in kingdom power, as seen by our faith and its foundation. Whenever we grasp the full scope of faith and act upon it, there will be effects in the circumstances and atmosphere around us. There will also be effects in the lives around us.

Effects of the kingdom are ultimately positive but also powerful in the establishing of the principles and ways of the kingdom. Jesus' everyday life and actions were lessons in the way of life for a person birthed into the Kingdom of God.

We couldn't just give these principles and ways a nod. They have to be lived out through every aspect of life. He is Lord of everything. He wants the kingdom to be established not just in our religious lives but in all of who we are. No matter what we think or are involved in, we are to have it centered on faith.

He didn't establish a set of rules or laws, as many would have us believe. He came to establish a kingdom built of love. Love is the essence and Spirit of God, and where that Holy Spirit is, there is a freedom that cannot be measured (2 Corinthians 3:17). Every aspect of life was and is based upon this faith, and our lives are to be established on it.

Jesus stood there and spoke with strength and authority. After His effectual command over the tree, ending its fruitlessness, He showed His desire to not just control but have responsibility of all around Him. He didn't just have authority over all things; He took responsibility for all things. Turning to His disciples, He simply stated:

"Have faith!"

He expected fruit, and there was none. He walked up to many people, expecting fruit of His love, and He found none. Fortunately, He didn't curse us as He did the tree. He poured more love on us. He limited His exercise of authority on us. He opened more opportunity for us to realize our own faith and authority.

As in the parables that Jesus told, there is always more to it than what can be understood and seen at first hearing or reading. Like here, He wasn't just showing the authority of a believer over nature by cursing the tree. He showed the expectation of the kingdom to be a person of faith.

There are those who might wonder about the symbolism of Jesus' choosing a fig tree and other items of the story. There could be speculation as to the prophetic nature of this act. But that is not the purpose of this writing; our focus is on Jesus and the faith He wielded in this act of power. The focus is the faith He told those around to hold. It is by faith that we live and with which we bring Him pleasure.

This single act would seem a negative act with long-lasting positive outcome. It should put into question our own faith. We need to ask ourselves how we have made use of our faith and the God-possibilities we have or haven't released. We have been entrusted with a great gift— faith. Only love stands greater than faith (1 Corinthians 13:13). The act of our faith is an act of our love.

Love is the power and the motivation that transformed God to man. It is love that draws our attention. Love focuses our vision of Him. Our faith becomes targeted by our vision of Him. Proverbs 29:18 tells us that we will perish without vision; we need to also realize without love we will perish. The life of faith focuses our love to His love.

Faith is the focal point of this lesson by Jesus. In cursing the tree and then demanding faith in those who followed Him, He was making a statement of kingdom proportion. Jesus' declaration to "have faith" was like the beginning of opening the gates into the kingdom. He swung open the land of the kingdom to the greatest adventure we could ever be a part of.

In this one act, He stretched into nonexistence any boundaries one might have concerning the Kingdom and faith. His Love knows no boundaries in His relationship with us, as we rise by faith through His glory (Ephesians 3:16–19). The common church has been trying to get outside the walls, when an activation and exercise of their faith would eliminate the walls altogether.

God should no longer be put in a box of what we are comfortable in believing. God will eliminate the box to help our faith rise to its full potential. He started our lives in a garden that had no boundaries. It was not until we rebelled and lost our faith that boundaries were added—those were to keep us out.

We can be faith's worst enemies by the limits we set. The box we have created only stifled our faith to see what God was able to accomplish through us. God is too big for a box, though we are not.

We box ourselves in by limiting ourselves from stretching out our faith to the extent God intended for us. By limiting our life experiences to that which is only flesh, we miss an entire kingdom. The Kingdom of God is a faith-driven venture that bridges the flesh and the spirit together.

We have become blinded by fleshly limits that make our inabilities seem greater than God's ability. Many modern teachings on faith expand the limits we place on God. Rather than enjoying the limitless glory of God, we tend to tolerate those things that we can hold in our hands. There is more to a walk of faith.

There are things of faith that define not only kingdom living but the very nature of our relationships in Christ. He demands more than for us to hold something; He requires us to stand in the nature and appointment of Christ. An active and strong faith transforms us into His image. In this transformation, we become like Him. The weak and bent person we were no longer exists; it is in the fading memory of a soul in need of retraining.

We do not just believe in order to go to heaven; we believe for the wholeness of our families, friends, communities, and the world. But most of all we have faith for His good pleasure. We believe; we have faith; we watch the Father in order to be like Him—not for any reason but for Him. Too many are more concerned about the world than they are about God.

There is no need for apologies for being a person of faith; the fruits of our faith will explain it all. There is no compromise for those of faith. We believe; we have faith; we know the truth. We stand as we should in His presence. Everything pales to His light and love.

We are to be what we are called to be (1 Peter 2:9). The Father set the standard by His own example. This is a reason for His saying to us, "Follow me!" (Matthew 16:24 NASB). Whether He was before a fruitless fig tree or beside the funeral pyre of the widow's son (Luke 7:12–16), the word spoken and acted on had an effect and influence upon everyone around.

Jesus' ability to see God and to hear God allowed Him to insert Himself into others' lives and change things to a kingdom standard of faith. His giving of Himself for us gave us the faith again to see and hear Him. We too, by faith, can make a difference and establish the kingdom of God.

He was not just making pronouncements; He was causing the very effect to happen by faith in Himself. The things Jesus did we also should be doing (John 14:12). Our word spoken in faith is the Spirit and life of the kingdom, because it is from the heart of the Father and once activated, there are results.

God's word is always creative. Our word, when spoken in ourselves, will not accomplish anything until it is the Word of God, spoken by faith. His word spoken in the beginning of creation—"Let there be" (Genesis 1 NASB); His word on the cross—"It is finished!" (John 19:30 NASB); and His command after His resurrection—"Reach for Him" (John 20:26–31)—still speak in power today. They are words of faith that lives.

Jesus, as the Word, having become flesh, gave witness by His actions of faith to who He was and to who we were to be. He was there in the beginning, and He, as the Word, speaks on forever. He was a man of authority, as seen in the healing of the centurion's son (Matthew 8:5–13). It is not enough to say something' that word must have power to do something.

As at the time of creation, that word of creation still releases the power of creation. Knowing that God's word does not return without power, we need to search for the word of the moment. His word is never empty of results or life.

Jesus, as the Word, has revealed Himself for us to follow into a new creation. A creation full of life and possibilities is full of power. Faith is full of revelation of the heart of the Father.

If you are going to be of faith, you must exhibit faith. There are no rewards for titles, only glory for the Father for obedience. There will be only emptiness for those who have chosen to allow their faith to lie dormant. It is though they exhausted themselves in their first act of faith, having believed for salvation. That was only the beginning of the act of creation, making us into a "new creation."

As the first of believers, Jesus reveals the power and necessity of faith. He also reveals the power of the Word. There is also an influence of need exposed in the fact that Jesus didn't find what He wanted.

Those around Him were awed when the tree died; for others, the focus was on what happened to a fruitless life. Everyone's focus delivers its own priority. By focusing on Jesus, we will be filled by the vision of Him and His glory. Our focus on Him will illuminate the path we are to take, and that path always leads to Him. He is the Word (John 1:1); and the Word is a lamp and light to show the way of faith and His will (Psalm 119:105).

The real focus should be on Jesus, with a realization of what He passed to each believer. He made it possible, through all He did, for us to know how to be used by this faith in order to please the Father. Believers through faith see less of themselves and their own needs and see more of the Father and the pleasure that their relationship and faith bring to Him. Our needs are met through meeting His need of fellowship and pleasure from us.

Through focusing on Him, all our needs are met. We need less because of having more in Him. The focus should be on where and how we, as believers, stand before the Father. We need to understand the change that comes in our adoption by God through faith. We are no longer strangers but family. We are children of God.

If we are not in a right position, then we cannot see the Father. We run the risk of missing another great moment of creation. We will not hear the incredible words of pleasure, "It is very good!" (Genesis 1:31). In those words, the kingdom is established in the hearts and community of man.

The Father has opened the kingdom to us and all it holds is for us. It is up to us to grasp it and allow Him to grasp us with all that is for us—and that is done by and with faith. It is in faith we live, (Romans 1:17) and are justified by it (Romans 3:27–28). "So then faith is awakened by our hearing, and we are to hear the Word from Christ" (Romans 10:17).

If Christ is the Word, then it is Him we are to see and follow as proof of our intimate lives with Him, through the faith He gave us.

Faith is not just in the word spoken; it is the power behind the releasing of the word, which manifests life into the situations and circumstances around each believer. We can no longer tell the world that Jesus is the answer; we must show them that He is the answer. There is a need of reality, a demonstration of His power, as we rely on the faith given to us by Him.

Faith is not a spoken word.

Faith can be revealed or activated by a spoken word. There have been enough sermons preached to save the world—if that was going to save the world, then there have been enough to save the world many times over again.

An act of faith is better proof than any verbal argument or treatise of the Father's love and care for all. Just as the Word is alive and powerful; so must our faith be alive and powerful. A healing, miracle, or sign and wonder, as an act of faith, shows the love of God in a greater manner than telling someone she or he is loved. Meeting any need by faith shows the presence and love of the Father.

Faith is not words spoken but love in action, to change and bless an individual and the world around us. It took one act on the cross and from the grave to prove God's love for the world; it will take one act of faith to show His love is still offered. There will need to come an understanding of faith and its use.

An act of faith is the power for us to show to a world that is out of control that there can be order out of its chaos. Faith granted us a relationship and access to the Father; it is the Father who will give us what we need in faith (Romans 12:3). He will continue to do so as we continue to obey. Obedience requires us to see Him and to react to Him and then act on His behalf (Psalm 123).

Faith allows us and those around us the opportunity of a great experience.

The greatest experience any can have and what most want is an experience and/or encounter with God. At the moment of that experience, we know Him as He wants to be known.

We are given an even greater opportunity to draw even closer to Him and be more like Him. If we would just look up to Him, we would gather understanding and revelation. All this happens and is given to us because of the Father's heart, which is poured out on us. He wants you and me to know our place with Him and the great benefit it is to the world (2 Timothy 2:11–12; Revelation 22:5).

His love is for us now, and His kingdom is established in us now by our acts of faith in Him. By acting on faith, we can then establish the kingdom in others and in our communities. If we want to change our communities for Christ, we must be first changed into the image of Christ.

Each act of faith brings the reality of the love of Christ closer to us and to those around us. In each act, they see Him and not us. Life was not intended to point to ourselves but to Him. We were not created so that we would exist; we were created in order for us to bring Him pleasure as we act in faith.

Faith is not just for the hereafter but for the present.

Faith is for the here and now.

He will not require of us what is not in us. "Have faith!"—it was more than a demand for what we should be using; it was an offering of what we should have and be.

"Have faith!"

Authority of faith is not for the enslavement of those around us but for the freedom of correctness or righteousness in Him. Faith isn't for what we do not have; it is for Him to inject His kingdom in and through us into others. We are infusing others not just with words but with the very Spirit of God that produces the faith needed to please Him.

There is an importance to the relationship between God and man. This is a combination of fruitfulness, blessing, and pleasure into which we enter by believing in Him. In having faith in Him, we choose to surrender all we are in order for Him to live in and through us (John 12:24; Galatians 2:20; Romans 12:1–3).

Nothing is held back from Him when we have faith. The person we were intended to be becomes more pronounced by this simple act of faith. He is Lord of all that we are now and are yet to be. Sometime in the relationship, we should appropriate the statement of John the Baptist as a prayer for our lives: "He must increase but I must decrease" (John 3:30 NASB).

It is not about our desires but about His desires. The entire act of creation and now re-creation has always been about Him. He did this for Himself. As much as we needed Him, He had a desire for our fellowship to be restored. This desire became a need in Him. He needs us in His presence, just as we need Him in our lives. He is more than a jealous God (Exodus 20:5); He is a God with needs.

In Him, we reflect and feel the heart of Him who now possesses us, indwells us, and fills us (Romans 8:11; 2 Timothy 1:9). A king demands nothing less than sacrifice, submission, and complete obedience. Our heavenly Father, the King of Kings will demand nothing less from us.

In return, He gives us His love, care, and protection. There is no greater reaction and fulfillment to our faith than that.

We have died to self, and now we illuminate the world by His great light and love, according to the faith given us. It is now that we realize what Paul expressed when he said, "It is not me who lives but God in me" (Galatians 2:20, author's paraphrase). When people see us, they see Him in us and hear the word of His life, playing and speaking through us.

By faith we are re-created into His image, as was intended from the very beginning. We see Him as the example and pattern for our lives. In seeing Him as He wants to be seen, we begin to pattern our lives into Him, as He re-creates us to show His image. Our faith, which is our ability to see Him, opens our life to God and His powerful love.

We can see that Jesus' reliance on the Father is what made Him able to do all He did, not the fact that He was the Son of God. Jesus had prayed for His disciples, in John 17:21 that we would be as the Father was in Him and as He was in the Father. To see Jesus was to see the Father (John 14:7–11). For others, it should be the same—to see us should be to see the Father.

The more we decrease, the more He will increase in the sight of others (John 3:30). Jesus was hiding in the cloak of love the Father gave Him (Colossians 3:14). The deeper our faith, the greater the revelation of who He is in us and the easier it is to live that revelation. If we can't live what we believe; it is not worth believing or activating our faith for.

Our relationships with the Father is based upon His work. Even the faith that we used to open our lives to His justification is based upon what He gave us (Romans 12:3). To some, it would seem that there is much to give up, but there is even more to gain in this relationship—we become real. We are seen as we should be seen: "in His image" (Genesis 1:26).

Some would believe that it is for our benefit, but it is actually for Him. We are created to bring Him pleasure (Ephesians 2:10). God was looking for a way to share His great love, a place to activate faith and to give hope. This space and time was to become a playground for God and a test field for the faith we were to be given.

Because we pawned our rightful place and authority, we had a large debt. He paid the price so that we could have fellowship with Him. He wanted to be with us and so paid the price of redemption for that which hid from Him in its shame for the loss—us in sin (Genesis 3). When the price was paid, all was restored to us, even our faith.

Even though it was our debt, it was for His love for us that He took it for His own. He wanted us with Him. He missed His walks with us and the face-to-face conversations. He wanted our faith reactivated so we would no longer hide ourselves. It did not matter to Him that we were wrong. It only mattered to Him that we would be made right again.

Jesus taught us how to live. He gave us an example of living in the kingdom and holding kingdom faith. Even in His death, we were given the lessons of faith and life. He showed us that we were to live a life of faith by doing as He asked.

"Follow me" (Mark 8:34 NASB) was a simple request.

Here is His word to allow the Word of God to dwell in us and what is expected (John 15:1–13). He was showing how man would have dominion over creation by the exercise of the faith of Jesus (Romans 3:22). People have complicated the simplicity that Jesus offered—"Have faith!"

In each miracle, healing, and sign or wonder, Jesus showed us the reach of our faith and authority. There was no limit but what we set. It was as though those things that caused such awe were actually supposed to be common—not that they wouldn't bring awe to us but that they would be more a part of our lives and who we are.

The awe will always be there when we realize the revelation of Him that we have.

No matter the setting, no matter the city, Jesus would find someone with enough faith to let things happen. No matter the day, He would meet someone's need. Circumstances did not rule what Jesus did; He ruled the circumstances.

There was no measure or standard of when to use faith. It was standard operating procedure to always live to the highest that our faith would show us. Just as everyone was able to see Him in action and the word of His actions spread, those actions are to continue today so that all can see Him now, and the news will spread as before, and all will come to believe in Him.

This is true and effective evangelism—a life of faith. Faith in action brings others to salvation, into a personal relationship with our God and Father. This could be an explanation of why we read so often in Scripture the simple phrase (or something similar) "and He healed many" (Mark 1:34 NASB); it was not to be the exception but the rule.

FAITH: THE GOD-POSSIBLE

The Example of Faith

Life is full of God-possibilities that will awe people into the Kingdom. We must be careful to not fall into a cursed life by being unfruitful. To feel the power was to experience the heart and love of the Father. To love the Father is to do His commandments (John 14:23–24).

Scripture tells us that the world could not contain the number of books that could be written on all He did and taught (John 21:25). The sound teaching and performing of miracles, signs, and wonders was not just a part of what He did but a part of who He was.

He did those things not only to bless others but to give us all a taste of the kingdom. In the Kingdom were to be new freedoms and experiences, open to all. It was not intended for us to read about the kingdom, but it is the intention of the Father for us to experience the Kingdom. We are not visiting a theme park; we are establishing the Kingdom of God for life.

Every step, word, and action is to be a reflection and reaction to the nudging and revelation of the Kingdom of God.

Our faith touched by the kingdom can only bring a reaction of power. The power of the resurrection is also the power of new life, showered by the love of God (Romans 8:11). Each miracle that was performed was an act of love, and God is love (1 John 4:7–8).

We are to share the love of the Father with the world that is in need of much love, and the greatest show of love is to lay down our lives (John 15:13). Then having done so, the resurrection power (Philippians 3:10) will manifest and touch many. We will not resurrect as the old self but as the "new self" (2 Corinthians 5:17). We will not be ourselves; we will be more like Him (1 John 3:2).

Just as in the days of Jesus, our very lives should be an act of showing God to others. Jesus was here to reveal the Father to us (John 14:6–7). We, in turn, should show the Father to a world that is searching and in need of a relationship with its heavenly Father, which is beyond any words and any good feelings (2 Corinthians 3:2–3). Our very lives read as the story of redemption when we allow our faith to touch the heart of God, bringing power into our everyday lives.

We act in faith so that His love may be known in the entire world. We act to the beat of His heart in order that He would be known by all who see Him in us. Our faith and each act of faith are testimonies of the faithfulness and mercy of our God. We do what we do and live as we live in order to bring pleasure to the heart of the Father.

His greatest pleasure in us is the fellowship He has with us. The fellowship between us and the Father allows our faith to bridge the realities of the Kingdom. Our faith brings the incredible powers and revelation of God into everyday existence.

An act of faith is a show of power.

It is a test of vision and a divine principle of life and the kingdom. It is not a matter of self-gain but of kingdom establishment. We were not given faith to build our kingdom; we were given faith to facilitate the establishing of His kingdom. We no longer live to our own hungers and thirsts but to His will (1 Peter 4:1–2).

When we believe it is no longer about us, it all becomes about Him. We reap the benefit of being "in Him:" all of the kingdom riches and glory (Ephesians 3:21); all that is necessary for our "life and godliness" (2 Peter 1:2–4 NASB). We benefit from the pleasure of pleasing Him. There is a constant reminder that it is about Him and not about us.

There is no free will once we surrender to Him; there is only His will and the power of our faith to affect those around us. It now is a will of freedom. We no longer seek our way, but in faith and by faith, we pursue His way of the kingdom (Matthew 6:33). We will see more of His manifestation when we allow our faith to make contact with His heart.

Jesus showed us that faith was not something to struggle with but the substance by which we live. If you will pray and activate the faith of Christ that He gave us, impossibilities become God-possibilities. With faith, we can move mountains, raise the dead, and so much more than any of us can imagine.

Active faith pleases God.

With faith, every day is full of His presence and the answers for life. A believer living by faith will experience a manifestation of His glory (Isaiah 35). When faith is made manifest, so is the grace and mercy of God. It is at that time we see the fulfillment of His vision and heart.

The statement, "a believer living by faith," is almost redundant. You can't be a believer without faith; only by faith do you become a believer. This is not a club you join and to which you claim membership, even though you never attend a meeting. It is not, as we see today, joining a church but not living as He calls us to do.

It was never intended to be about joining a common church; it was to be about Him and the faith He gave us.

Our first act of faith was the labor pains of the born-again experience. A child of the Kingdom is born by the light of faith. The new birth is a process of being translated from the kingdom of darkness into the kingdom of Light. This is one of the greatest miracles and shows of power there can be—moving between realities of the kingdom, through space and time, just as the Father did for us, to restore us to Him.

This is but the first step in the life of the kingdom that is lively with faith. The incredible life of the kingdom citizen manifests the maturation of faith and thinking. The more we are able to activate and exercise our faith, the more we walk the lifestyle.

Our faith brings about the manifestation of the Kingdom of God in our lives.

God calls us and provides the power and ability to respond, which is our faith. So by faith we live and are made whole. Our realization of salvation may be progressive, but at the moment, we believe we are wholly saved. Salvation isn't in parts, nor is it parted out. Jesus paid the full price on the cross. He is not making payments.

We are surrounded by God-possibilities—the Kingdom of God is alive with them. This is how we live and how we are sustained and move (Acts 17:28). It is all by faith. It is by faith that we live (Romans 1:17). The life of faith is to be the rule, not the exception.

Every moment of our lives is a moment of God-possibilities through active faith. Our born-again experiences have opened the kingdom and all that it holds for us, which now can be seen and known. This is a reason to explain why Jesus could tell us to ask for anything, and it would be given to us.

Now, we should ask ourselves, "Has there been a second or even a third or fourth act of faith manifested in our lives? Is our faith dead or vital?"

For some, that may be enough, and it may be—if it were just about our getting to heaven. The reality is that our active faith is for the Father to fellowship with us. He gave us our faith in order to draw nearer to us. He wants our faith to reveal the total of his great love in us. He wants us to look into His eyes and not away from His gaze.

It is time that we realize that all He has done was done for Him, not us.

For any believer to try to maintain a lifestyle is to eventually fall back, unless his or her faith is renewed and recharged. There must be growth in order to hold fast. We are called to maturity. All the gifts are given to help in that maturation process (Ephesians

4:11–17). Our maturity is the process of revealing the goodness within that He breathed into us in the beginning.

We can fight the plan of God, or we can live the life that He gave us—the faith to attain and demonstrate a life in His presence. There are those who make more of being a part of the world than being in the presence of God. Our worship to Him is not what we do before the world but how much we pay attention to Him. We shouldn't fight Him; we must yield to Him.

A believer will want to do all he or she can to please the Father and to be with the Father. A walk and life of faith is the way for a growing believer to make sure he or she is at the heart of the Father. As we grow to maturity, we see opportunities for faith.

Let's not make the mistake of thinking that maturity is being grown up. Remember that Jesus said that it is as a child that we enter the Kingdom (Mark 10:15). We are to show childlike attitudes, love, and devotion toward Jesus and His ways. Jesus, at times, purposely chose children to teach us a principle or concept of kingdom living and faith.

Our hearts and devotion belong to the Father. We should feel joy, not any hurt, anger, or hatred. Look into His face, and you will see the love that may have been missing from an earthly parent. He wants to have fun and enjoy our lives with us (John 15:11). There is healing, satisfaction, and wholeness when we act on faith and not on feelings. Faith brings our emotions to greater heights and sensitivity.

Our lives of faith—or the lack of it—could be what separates others from the kingdom. That is to say, our dead faith may block others from entering the Kingdom of God, because they do not see a difference between our lives and what they are experiencing themselves. Why would someone attempt to believe what we believe, if it isn't making a difference in our own lives?

There are those that say they have faith but many cannot prove it beyond the words they say. Faith must be strong and active, or it is of no use. Why should a person exercise something that has not made a difference or has been seen as ineffective?

People look at our lives to see what Christ has done for us and therefore what He can do for them (2 Corinthians 3:2–3). They turn to doctors and their drugs, because they see an effect. They turn to witchcraft and such, because they see a difference. Those who can show their life is different and strong get the most attention and the most converts.

Living life as a believer is more than just living up to someone's behavioral standards. It is easy to choose the rules to live by and say we meet the standard. Rules are easy to state, and therefore we can easily declare ourselves as having met the standard.

Our standard—our goal, our easy plan to succeed—is a roadblock to our kingdom life. We must have only His way and plan, which is the only and best way for real kingdom citizens. It is best that we step back and follow Him, with the focus totally on Him and not on us. This is a reminder that it is about Him, not us.

Being a believer is more than doing the "right" things or behaving the "right" way.

Faith exposes the Father to us, and one glimpse of Him erases all self-standards. We then just pursue Him and His heart, and we quickly discover that it isn't about what we do but who

He is. He sees the beginning and the end as one. His directions lead us to the maturity and blessing to which He has called us.

It is amazing to step into His light and see all the blessings we have in faith, rather than the "dark glass" of partial revelation on which many rely (1 Corinthians 13:12). He is no longer hidden from us, nor do we hide from Him. We have full access to Him, His promises, and His love. We now walk side by side and talk face-to-face with Him.

Active faith is the difference and is the constant in a believer's life. Being a believer is "being in Him," and our lives are to show Him and not us (John 15). There are no more impossibilities, as all are God-possibilities. Faith takes us out of the common and into the incredible world of the real. The "real" is that life in our flesh being infiltrated and controlled by the Spirit.

We then go from being ruled by our circumstances to being the ruler of this world and life. We shouldn't wait for another life after this; we should allow the Holy Spirit to flood through us so that the flesh is under the authority of the Spirit. We enjoy through our bodies all the blessings of the Father. Our activated and lively faith can lead many to the kingdom through faith in Christ.

Our faith changes our behavior, so that our lives are an example of having a whole life of joy and peace. This is a life of faith and a relationship through faith. Through faith, the relationship between God and any individual becomes the new focus. Others begin to see and feel the power of our faith. They see the God-possibilities by our steadfastness in the faith. We have melded flesh and Spirit by our faith.

People want to know what that relationship is worth. If it is worth as much as we claim, have we pursued it with all we are or have? They want to know if we believe what we say. They want to know that there is something to believe in, that there is something there that is different from what they believe in now. They want to know if it is worth the exchange.

The capacity of faith to which we are called is the capacity of complete sacrifice that Jesus showed us can be made. We are to believe with our whole selves. Our faith is to consume our entire beings. If it is by this consuming faith that we are saved and should live, then we should be consumed by the giver of faith.

Faith becomes part of the purpose, power, and potential of a kingdom life.

In Matthew 13:44–46, Jesus tells the parable about two men selling all they had in order to possess a treasure and a great pearl. He was talking about the Kingdom of God. Faith helps us see the treasure as real, for we possess more of the capacity we are called to live and share.

Faith is of the Kingdom of God, and it must be possessed.

The honor we show by our faith is an incredible light in the darkness for those who are searching and may be lost. The light of a soul is ignited by the faith we put toward correcting our relationships with God. God finds great pleasure as our faith brings us closer to Him. Our faith makes us more of Him and less of self.

Your relationship, not your behavior, is the difference in your life that will attract others to Him. Behaviors can be learned, and so they can be deceptive. A true relationship with God in faith cannot be faked; it exhibits the highest of life and righteousness.

Out of our personal relationships with Him comes all that there is about being a believer. Many would show you a list of statements, a calendar of events, or a receipt of giving, and point to them as acts of their relationship. Those should be only symptoms of the real relationship of sacrifice, which is love. Our faith brings us into obedience to the events of the cross.

We sacrifice ourselves in order to be like Him.

The real act of our relationships, the very being of believers, is laying down all we are for another.

It is about living by faith and not by our own works.

It is allowing Him to flow through us, not our choosing what we do for Him.

Faith will keep the focus on Him, as we see and receive more revelation of His heart and self.

Paul said, "It is no longer I who live but Christ that lives in me" (Galatians 2:20 NASB). God is calling us to no longer live for ourselves but to live for Him. He died for us, so that we can have a relationship with Him. Our faith makes this relationship real.

Are we so arrogant to think that we are saved so that we will avoid hell? We are allowed salvation so that we might fulfill our purpose of pleasing Him. We are created to have fellowship with Him. We didn't create Him so that He can have fellowship with us.

There has to be a new mind-set and a redefining of how this works. This is godly repentance. Faith isn't used for what we can get but for who He is. There is both potential and possibilities in us, according to our faith. We need to feel free to exercise our faith to find the potential of our faith, so that we know the way of bringing the greatest pleasure to God. It is in the fullness of faith that we have His greatest pleasure in sight. It is all for His praise and glory.

This is a faith that reveals and highlights our relationships in and with Christ.

In this relationship of faith comes knowledge of Him that reveals His power. Here is power for living life to His glory and honor. We are not the center; Christ is the true center of all things to which we are drawn. He is more than the sustainer of all things. He is the definition of these things (Colossians 1:15–20).

Through God's great grace and mercy, by which He gave this faith, we see and know the power that gives all "things that pertain to life and godliness" (2 Peter 1:3 NASB). Only then can we begin to understand the incredible love that He has for us. His mercy and grace and all the attributes contributed to Him begin to transform our beings and character—literally, all that was us.

We must learn to trust that He knows best. Our ability to live by faith is partially a matter of trust. We have to have trust, which is just one part of what constitutes our faith. Jesus knows what is best, even if we do not see the full picture of where He is taking us.

It is hard for many to let go of their life into the hands of another, even if it is God. But if we would let ourselves understand a simple fact—He sees and knows more than us—the Father's perspective of our lives can mean radical change for us and our communities.

The impact that a confrontation with the glory of God can have on us and others is immeasurable. We cannot stoop to the silliness to which so many have fallen—counting heads for a church service or noting the size of our bank accounts. It is all about Him, who is the focus and author of our faith (Hebrews 12:1–3).

There is no time to draw attention to oneself; there is only time to bow before Him. The lower we bow, the higher He is able to arise and illumine His ways. The more He is revealed, the greater the God-possibilities. People do not have time or life enough to wait for us to get our act together or to grow out of the way. They need our faith to activate and reveal the path of this kingdom relationship.

Faith shapes our lives.

Faith shapes our view of life.

Faith can cause or prevent things that have the potential to direct or redirect our lives.

Faith, even when it is not active, by its very inaction shapes our lives, usually in a negative way. The relationship that we have with the Father based upon *faith* is not about what we can get but about what we have in Him. It is about what we are to Him. The greatest part is that it is Him we have and He has us.

When we relax in our relationships with Him, the possibilities before us become realities. Our faith becomes the pigment to the paint of life. There is no "figment of the imagination" but a tangible reality of the now of the flesh and Spirit.

I have heard people declare many times that they had did not receive something from God because of their lack of faith. I have always wondered how they knew that it was a lack of faith and why they didn't change that situation in order to have their faith fulfilled. A person generally doesn't spend money from a bank account that has insufficient funds, unless there is intentional deceit on the part of the spender.

In reality, it is the lack of activation or the lack of life of our faith that causes these lapses.

It is also a matter of the persons not understanding what the Father may have for him or her. When we tie God's hands to do only what we want, it usually results in nothing. That is not faith. Making a list of demands that only feed our desires is not faith; it is a definite sign of immaturity.

Faith is seeing and acting upon what He wants, on what He does and says.

This is very much what Jesus was saying when He declared that He only did what the Father had commanded or shown to Him (John 8:26–29, 38). There cannot be any argument that the life of Jesus was challenging and revolutionary to those that chose to follow Him. He showed us how much the Father wanted to restore faith and fellowship.

We need to learn that a truly surrendered life that is experiencing His constant presence will not ask for or seek what cannot be given or done, nor does it ask for that which we shouldn't have asked.

Faith keeps things stirred.

We no longer look at the impossibilities but at the God-possibilities.

Faith is to be alive and active. By faith we will see the world change and come into alignment with the Kingdom of God.

I can tell stories of how faith made the difference—my and my family's personal experiences. God kept our faith alive and vital as He showed Himself faithful to my family and me. Though I might not have made the most of the opportunity, as I wish I had, He continued to make Himself real to me and gave revelation of life in the Kingdom.

I once had a terrible infection in my kidneys and urinary tract, and nothing was helping or improving the situation. The symptoms persisted for weeks. The doctors did not know the cause, but they knew it was serious, for the kidneys were not working properly. Their prognosis was not good.

During this time, I attended a revival service and heard a sermon on faith. I realized that I had allowed my faith to take a back row in my life and ministry. Immediately, I stood and walked in front of the evangelist for prayer, but before anything could happen, God took over. My faith was rewarded by healing. From that exact moment on, the health problem stopped.

On another occasion, my family was given notice to move from our house that we had rented for the past four years. We had been hit with a financial disaster, however, and could not afford to move. With one dollar in our savings account and thirty dollars in our checking account, we prayed and searched for a home. All anticipated income was spent on bills and groceries.

Within the next two-plus weeks, we found a house, and over three thousand dollars came in to pay for the move, deposits, and the first month's rent. It wasn't about missing the disaster but about Him walking us through it.

Faith was the only constant in our life.

Our faith was given an opportunity to open up and be seen. I am not saying we took proper advantage of the opportunities, but our faith is stronger and ready for what He calls us to and shows us. No matter what others think, if we had not activated and used our faith, we would not have been able to do what we did.

You may say that these acts of faith brought things to us. Actually, these acts of faith changed my family and me. We do not see life as we used to. We try our best to make sure that everything is done according to Him and His leading. Others will always see the negative, and if they don't see it, they make it up as they look over someone's life. Our focus must remain on Him, and that is our faith. It has never been about us but always about Him.

Our faith is our obedience at the sight of Him.

Our faith is the reality of the relationship dynamics we have with God our Father. We abide in Him and most important, He abides in us (John 15:1–11). In that relationship, there is no separation, and He is dominant in the life that we live in kingdom style.

We have found that living by faith gives guidance to living a life from which He can receive glory. It definitely is a different mind-set to have. It requires persistence to see it worked through. It has to be lived out in every aspect of our lives. There is no holding anything back of ourselves; it has to be given and lived for Him in us.

My faith transforms and grows, the more I rest in Him.

Let me share another's story and the faith by which he lived. In each church service, the organist and/or pianist played the chorus to the hymn "Only Believe":

> Only believe, only believe,
> All things are possible,
> Only believe.

It was a signal to some and encouragement to others that a man of faith was there and would soon come to the platform to pray for them. William Branham (1909–1965) confessed to only being a man, although others called him a prophet. No matter what you thought of the preacher, God would show up in response to the faith he and others had in the building and people were healed.

William Branham's ministry led to controversy in the later years, but no one who was there could deny the power of faith wielded by him. You can read accounts of his life in other books, but the stories are nearly endless—of cancer being healed, tumors falling off people, and even those dead rising to life. He would always ask the person to believe in Jesus Christ, and the miracles would take place.

There are many names that can be thrown out to you— Oral Roberts (1918-2009), Kathryn Kuhlman (1907–1976), F. F. Bosworth (1877-1958), A. A. Allen (1911-1970), Charles Price (1887-1947), Maria Woodworth-Etter (1844-1924), Amie Semple McPherson (1890-1944), Vickie Jamison (1936-2008), Benny

Hinn (1952-present), John Wimber (1934-1997), and Randy Clark (1957-present), just to name a few. During the healing revival of the 1950s, there were over 250 healing evangelists traveling the United States. All of these can testify to instances that when faith was activated at any capacity, things took place that could only be explained as God acknowledging the people's faith.

Faith was electric and contagious to many.

Another to mention is Smith Wigglesworth (1859–1947), whose rough ways were known all over the world—when he saw evidence of sickness or disease, he would slap or punch the person and then see the person healed, as tumors and cancers would fall off. He has been called the 'Apostle of Faith.' He was so convinced that faith was the key that if a healing did not manifest itself immediately, he declared there was a lack of faith.

John G. Lake (1870–1935) was another with incredible faith. He would allow doctors to examine patients as he prayed, so that they could monitor the difference in power as the healing took place. In the Healing Rooms of Spokane, Washington, which he opened in 1915, over 100,000 healings were documented in five years. The ministry was duplicated in Portland, Oregon, shortly after that.

He taught that faith was integral to seeing healing manifested.

Stories abound about the ministry of John G. Lake. His going to Africa as a missionary was an incredible step of faith. He did not have money or a place to live, but he packed up his family and went to Africa. As a need would come up, the answer would be close behind. His intense prayer life as well as his works among the sick and dying were all testimonies of a man of tremendous faith.

Stories of John G. Lake and his family going to Africa show God's provisions. Because Brother Lake heard from God to go to Africa, he knew God would provide. As he stood in line at customs, where he knew he would be asked if he had a specific amount of money (the amount that the government expected every person to have to stay in the country), a man stepped up to him and gave him the money needed to enter the country.

Neither did he know where he and his family would live. A woman was questioning different individuals as they came through the line. When she came to Brother Lake, and he answered her questions, she told him their house was ready— that God had told her to have it prepared and to come and bring them to it.

If you have ever been to a service in which Benny Hinn is ministering, you would know that he prays directly with few individuals. The atmosphere of worship combined with faith is an explosion of power as the Holy Spirit moves. Many testify of being healed as they waited, or as the choir sang, or as someone else was being prayed for.

An atmosphere rich in faith is rich with the presence of God and is a perfect place for all things to be made manifest— salvation, healing, and provisions. If we take time for Him, then He will lead us through steps and the path where our faith is the strongest.

Nothing is impossible when God is active (Luke 18:27).

We can't do it by ourselves, but He who is in us can, without limits. He gave the faith for us to see His ways and to know where His power was to be activated, for others to experience Him. Although some examples above may be controversial, we must learn to grasp the faith and avoid the controversy, if possible. If that isn't possible, we have to grasp faith. In all these things, we give God the praise and glory, for it is by Him that these things happen. Our faith puts us into position and alignment to His will and ways.

I recall several services in which testimonies were recounted of healing or other miraculous happenings. As people listened, their faith rose within them in anticipation of their own healing and miracle. There were individuals with all sorts of sickness and problems. There were people that exercised their faith with our ministry and received healing from cancer, tumors, back problems, headaches, and many other sicknesses.

I remember a service at a local church where Deborah and I spoke on faith and healing. It wasn't a large crowd but there were several who hoped to be healed and helped by God. That night, several gave testimony of God's touch. The testimonies that gave us the biggest thrill were those of individuals who started up to the front to receive ministry but went back to their seats, because they received their healing before making it to the prayer line. Their faith—not the ministry—caused them to receive their healing.

It is not just healing that takes place; provisions of all sorts have happened. Several years ago, a couple in our church, Howard and Barbara, told of their trip to Bible college. They had their entire life's savings in a shoebox—something like $362. They were going to put their faith and trust in God for all their needs.

As they traveled, they were frugal with their money, but whenever they had to pay for something, they reached into the box and took what they needed to pay their bills. Never during the trip did they stop to count what was left of their funds.

When they finally reached the Bible college, they settled in to their apartment. It was then they decided to count the money in the shoebox to see what, if anything, they might have left. They counted exactly $362—the amount they started with. Howard said he always wondered if the money would have continued to multiply if they had not counted it and just had continued to live their faith.

Countless other stories can be recounted that show how God responded to people's faith. He provided for them to accomplish what He required (Romans 12:3). Hopefully, through a better understanding of faith, we will have more living by it and activating others.

It is faith alone that we are asked to live by. "As we move from one faith experience to another, God's right way of living is revealed. As was recorded for us that to live right there must be faith" (Romans 1:17, author's paraphrase).

Just as there are more stories, there are more ways that faith can manifest itself in our lives and communities. We cannot limit the possibilities of what God may want to do in our lives to only those things with which we may feel comfortable. God has much to reveal to us.

Each experience with your faith builds on the experience before, so that your faith is stronger and more ready. In this process, you are able to see more clearly the path of the Father and even experience more of what faith can do with and through you. Our capacity increases as our experience grows. Our vision clears each time we exercise our faith. We draw closer to Him and become more like Him. At some point, He is all that is seen in us.

Many have been fixated on the personalities, rather than on God. Some would concentrate on methods or styles of an individual. Their sight needs to be upon the Father. Faith is increased and responded to when we focus on Him. Faith is only killed when the focus is on man and his methods, style, wording, or practice.

It is not the man or his style or any of that which brings the miracle. It is the connection that faith brings to our Father that opens the door for our healing or whatever the need may be.

We are sustained by His Word through His faith given to us. We see by faith that His plan always points to Him. It is in Him, our Lord and King that we understand if we follow Him we have all that is needed or wanted.

To look anywhere but to the Father by our faith is to run the risk of missing what the Father is doing or being—or worse, missing His look of pleasure and love toward us.

This misplaced focus can cause fear to arise rather than faith. Fear enters when we compare ourselves to others or because of our perception of the expectations of others. We fear we might not measure up, and so we ask, out of intimidation rather than boldness of our faith. We truly do not expect anything, and so we are not disappointed.

We do not receive when we ask in fear, but our doubts are fed. Doubt buries the sick, rather than conquering death.

Fear blocks faith.

There is not enough scriptural precedent to say there is a right or wrong way to use faith. Faith can only point or lead to Christ and the Father. Any other works are not faith but dead works.

When our faith is activated in any way, it will lead to the fulfillment of the Father's heart. Man is only the point of the activity within the equation of a true act of faith or an activation of faith. As has been said, the believer's life is not about the believer; it is about the Father and His Kingdom.

It is more than just saying, "We live by faith." We must walk faith throughout our lives. Faith isn't about our needs or desires but about His heart being touched and fulfilled. The misplacement of faith's focus could explain the mistrust that many have for the common church and "Christians." It is time for every believer to rise above the common and walk in the faith that he or she has been given, and show the "all" that God has for everyone in faith, hope, and love.

Psalm 37:4–5 says that He will give us the desires of our hearts. But could it not be better understood that when we have given ourselves totally to a life of faith, that His desires become ours? That would mean that we have come closer to the fulfillment of John the Baptist's statement: "He must increase, but I must decrease" (John 3:30 NASB).

Faith is a surrendering of ourselves to Him and His heart.

Faith is not the power or ability to manipulate God or anyone around us. We cannot force God to do anything He does not want to do. He may grant us something that is not the best in order to teach us a better way to live in our faith. And to manipulate others is to practice witchcraft; which is condemned in Scripture.

A true walk and life of faith is not about what we can do or have but about Him and what He has done. To fully grasp this relationship to the Father and the power of this faith is to cause an explosion of nuclear sorts into the lives of those around us.

The continual anticipation and boldness that we will live when faith is alive will be contagious. It will become easier to truly live as John the Baptist declared: "He must increase, but I must decrease" (John 3:30 NASB). Faith is integral to our becoming more like Him.

Faith is an important ingredient and the energy of our walk as a believer. We must learn and know how to use it, how to pass it on, and how to activate each other's faith. Here is our capability and ability to please Him.

Faith truly takes us from the realm of the impossible to the realm of all possibilities. Faith not only brings us into relationship with God, but it is integral to our continued relationships with the Father and the establishing the Kingdom of God around us (Hebrews 11:6). Faith makes all things happen and will reveal all things to us, as we focus on Him.

There is, in each of us, the ability to bring pleasure and joy to God. He gets the most pleasure from us for just who we are—His creation. Faith draws on our DNA, the essence of who we are. Faith will show the relationship we have with the Father.

The things we do, think, or try gives God pleasure, but just our being there with Him gives Him the greatest thrill. His love becomes the light of the moment in each heart. It is then that we explore the height, depth, and width of His love on wings of faith. He enjoys seeing the reflection of Himself in us, the vibration of our contact with Him.

His love for us is a powerful force in our lives. He pours His love on us no matter our circumstances of life. His love is not based on us; it is founded upon His heart and holiness. His very nature is to love, especially to love each of us (1 John 4:7–8). He does this in order to stir that which He gave us—our love and faith even more in Him.

By His love, He has given us faith in order for us to better enjoy Him and His love. Our faith is also given to us so that we might bring more praise and pleasure to Him. The Father wants us to enjoy the sight of Him as much as He enjoys the sight of us. It is as if the Father wants us to have a party. And we are His special guests.

Faith clears our vision.

Faith allows revelation and relationship to flow freely. Scripture tells us that "in His presence we are made free" (2 Corinthians 3:17, author's paraphrase). This is the same Holy Spirit that fans our faith and is the agent to fulfilling our faith. Faith clears the way so that it is no longer us looking "through a mirror dimly" (1 Corinthians 13:12 NASB). Jesus reveals to us all things so that we can have all the things He has promised, for us to be restored to His original intentions. There has always been a purpose to everything that takes place, and it is for our benefit and His pleasure.

Without faith, we only see ourselves. All concerns are for us. As children, we looked always at ourselves. As we matured, the mirror cleared to a window, and we began to see the Father and know His heart. The more we rely upon our faith, the fewer limits we have. No more mirrors, no more windows, and no more barriers—just the Father and us, face-to-face. When done under the influence and power of faith; those things considered supernatural become more natural.

The Father enjoys just being with us—there is no need for there to be anything going on. The greater His pleasure grows, the fuller our joy in Him. We draw our faith and life from the Father, as He reacts in pleasure to our obedience. He continues to make His deposits in us for His greater pleasure.

We "walk in the Spirit" daily by the power of faith.

Faith allows us the power and opportunity to enjoy this relationship. It gives us the sight and understanding to enjoy the moment to its fullest, because it is His moment. In that moment our freedom from the limits of who we are moves us into the limitlessness of who He is. It is this moment that those things unseen become more real.

Most acts of faith and belief are individual acts, not corporate. We activate our faith on behalf of someone or a group. It isn't the number of people who are praying that gets things done; it's the capacity of one's faith.

We see this in Daniel as he prayed for his nation (Daniel 10), and in Christ—whether in the garden or on the cross, it was one man's act of faith for a nation or the world (Romans 5:12–15). This is the same in many aspects as a believer's life. Groups of people came together for prayer and encouragement, but it was individual acts of faith that changed—or changes—the world.

You and I, as individual believers, become incredibly important to the plan of God.

This is not talking about how much God loves us; that can never change. Too many begin to doubt His love and thus question their own salvation, when it should never be a question for the believer. Our salvation is as secure as His love for each of us. He loves us with an "everlasting Love" (Jeremiah 31:3 NASB), a love from which we cannot be separated (Romans 8:35–39).

God loves you just because of who He is, not because of what you do.

You can't make God love you anymore than He does right now, whether you are a believer or non-believer. And even as important in the psychological circus of today, you cannot do anything that will make God love you any less. God loves you unconditionally, deeply and passionately.

His love is constant, true, and unchanging.

God loves you—let that settle into your soul and bring peace and joy. Then watch your faith grow. In your faith, you will find the ability and power to make the connection between you and God.

The love of God should be a settled point in our lives. We are talking of faith, which seems tested on a consistent basis. The tests come from many sources—internal and external; self-employed and from others. These tests come especially during our exercise of our faith, which in turn causes many to question the love of God for them. It is important that we change the tests to opportunities for our faith to manifest Him.

Exercise of a believer's faith is not an option.

The use and exercise of our faith is necessary and mandatory. It is simply stated, "Without faith we cannot please the Father" (Hebrews 11:6, author's paraphrase). In order to experience the free flow of the Father's pleasure, we will engage our faith. Finding that place of His pleasure is the place of our joy in Him.

It is an incredible feeling of peace and satisfaction, even abundant joy, when we find that place of pleasure for the Father— that place we seek and stand in is His presence, which is rich in faith, power and, most of all, His glory. The Kingdom of God is the place of His presence.

Within the Kingdom of God, His power is exercised easily and freely. His glory is the light and banner of the kingdom. We react and act upon the faith the King has given to us in His Kingdom. Being surrounded by such faith, it makes it easier to continue to rely and act on faith (Hebrews 12:1–3).

This Kingdom of God can be found within, according to Jesus (Luke 17:21). We are the dwelling place (1 Corinthians 6:19), the place of presence for the Father. He is on the throne of His kingdom. His Holy Spirit in us and us in Him brings pleasure (Romans 14:17). We can make this realization as we walk in and under the influence of the Holy Spirit; which has been given in answer to our faith in Christ.

We need to remember that He gave us our faith to use. In order to be with Him, our faith will enlarge our capacity and grow stronger, so that we can enjoy more of Him as He enjoys more of us. We must have faith to enter in and enjoy the benefits of the kingdom of God. The greatest benefit is Him and His continued presence. But there are many other benefits that we may have yet to enjoy, and we unleash our faith to experience His fullness.

Faith is a key of the kingdom that we must employ in order to be a part of the kingdom and to activate the kingdom life in and around us. We use this key as any other key—to open up the massive treasure of a Father's heart full of love and care for each of us. We enter to be embraced by Him, who enlarges our capacity for Him and all that He would have for us.

If we do not know what faith is, how can we be sure we have it? If we have never felt the surge of faith through us, how can we know it is working? Is it a matter of taking faith on faith?

There comes a point in the believer's life where each believer must come to grips with his faith and use it for something beyond himself. As a believer uses this faith, it will get more of a grip on the believer. A life of faith almost becomes an obsession. Nothing else matters but God's good pleasure.

A believer cannot afford to wait for the by-and-by to know that his salvation is complete. There is an assurance that comes from faith that helps know beyond knowing that we are kingdom citizens. A believer can experience and know a more complete salvation now. The waiting is upon the daily revelation of the Father, not in a time yet to be.

We need to get away from the thinking that it is all for another day and place. Salvation is for today (2 Corinthians 6:2). The Kingdom of God is here (Matthew 3:2). We wait so that we can experience something now. This becomes a critical moment of soul searching, of whether or not a life and time has been wasted.

A person's faith can come under question or be tested under many circumstances or reasons. Faith must stand the test of life and time. It must withstand the questions of reason or the attacks of the enemy. We are tested for what we have, not what we might not have. These are opportunities for Jesus to show us more of what He is capable of doing in and through us, when we have belief in Him.

Faith should not be stagnant or dead. Our faith is made alive by its use and by the Holy Spirit of God, which is the Spirit of life and righteousness within us. All things that relate in any way to our faith point to life, energy, growth, and power. We do not get the choice of the "when" or even the "how" of our opportunities for faith, but we must be ready to give an answer for our hope and faith (1 Peter 3:13–16).

Our faith is a gift that must be used and not set on a shelf to admire. The shelf is for the trophies won by employing the power of our faith in order to bring glory and praise to the Father, who sits on the throne of our heart and His kingdom. The Kingdom of God is a place of power and life, which both are empowered and activated by faith.

Our faith must bear the same characteristics as the Father and His kingdom.

What have we done with the gift that was given us? Which servant are we—the one who hid his talent or the one who spent it wisely (Matthew 25:14–30)? The servant that hid his talent lived in fear the whole time, but as a believer, faith and fear cannot coexist. Objects of fear are not from God. He only gives "good and perfect" gifts (James 1:17; 2 Timothy 1:7).

Those servants who used their talents and made gain enjoyed the presence of their Master. Each of them used his gift differently but effectively in his pursuit to please the Master. They recognized the opportunity for their character and the trust their Master showed them. The Master was pleased and benefited. His benefit became the blessing for the others.

The focus upon the Master and each servant's perception of Him was what led them to use or hide their talent. Those who followed His example were blessed; those who did their own thing lost everything. Their fear bound their faith and caused them to hide both faith and talents.

Our faith will encourage us to focus on Him, rather than on us or what we can do or gain. The gain is not ours; it is His. It's not how much but the fact that we did what He wanted. Many put faith to the test by comparing what has been won and gained in this world, rather than seeing the victories of the kingdom as the expansion of its principles and power into more and more lives around us.

We were warned about gain in the world and the cost to our soul (Matthew 16:26), so there is no comparison. Gain in the world can and will come to some, but that is not the measure of success. Faith's success is measured by the pleasure found in God's heart and will manifest itself through our own hearts.

The moving of the Holy Spirit in people's lives today is a stirring for more of the heart of God to be revealed in individuals. What is revived in this move is our faith—faith in Him and faith for His ways. That is why during revival, we see an increase in healings; signs, and wonders. Faith goes from a word or statement to an explosive action on the scene of the kingdom.

This is the time when no longer will it be acceptable to only declare having faith. It is time that the fruit of our faith is exposed, not just in a church or fellowship of believers but into every aspect of life around us. We do not believe and stand ready to exercise our faith for only a band of believers but for the world as a whole to see and believe. Every fellowship of believers should have the capacity of faith that drives them to kingdom living.

In the past, we saw that healing, signs, and wonders accompanied revival, renewal, awakening, and/or reformation. Faith was raised to a capacity where things happened. People became born again and began kingdom living. As people became comfortable and satisfied with their new place in the world, faith became less important and less used.

We have seen an increase of denominations and common churches as we have seen a decrease in healing, signs, and wonders. The decrease in faith led to a decrease in signs and wonders, which further eroded faith to a point where individuals quit believing signs and wonders could happen—and even denied that they ever had happened. The common church began to help people feel good instead of making people whole, through faith.

It is a form of selfishness to use our faith only so that we go to heaven, especially if we have heard and read the Word of God, which has called us to overtake the earth with the Kingdom of God. The acts of faith in which participate we in are about Jesus and His pleasure, not about us.

It is also selfishness to use our faith for personal gain and not a gain to increase our faith and kingdom influence in others. Selfishness has no part of real faith but faith has become a catch-word. Selfishness takes the attention away from the Father. Real faith is about the Father and puts all the attention on Him.

Faith changes things and makes things happen. Ask yourself this: "When was the last time my faith made someone stop and take notice?" If preaching caused the world to take note of the kingdom, there would be more believers, not just more churches or groups.

It is our honor and call to give others the experience of the love of God by allowing our faith to be activated on behalf of others. A true person of faith will act on others' behalf and seek God's pleasure, rather than just his own salvation. We can seek God by helping others to allow the manifestation of the Holy Spirit in their own life.

The believer is the representative of God to this world. Just as Jesus represented God to this world by healing, signs, and wonders, and love; so we must represent God in the same way. Jesus never thought of Himself; it was always about the Father and the Father's heart for us. We are not only called to give the world our faith, but we owe them this opportunity. So what is faith?

Faith is more than a declaration of a desire. You can declare a thing until your face turns blue, but until the thing is manifested, your faith hasn't been activated. You can stand in a garage and call yourself a car all day long, but until you grow wheels and an engine, you are not a car. This might have been an over-simplification, but it is true. There must be a power behind any declaration. There has to be a hope in something. Hope is only for those things that will be seen when faith is working. True faith is that power and ability.

Our faith comes from the Father as He reveals His will and way to us. It is not our choice of desires; it is our surrender to Him that gives clear direction and the use of our faith for such incredible results.

Faith is a spiritual power. Faith is the power to believe. It is the power to see and go beyond what is here and now. Faith is the power to obey the Father and see His will complete in our lives and in those around us.

Faith is at the heart of the Father for you and me as believers.

The Father's love is so strong for us that He has freely given to us what He has required for us to have an open relationship with Him. Faith is alive and growing in the believer who actively believes. It permeates every avenue of a person's life. All thoughts and activities are colored by faith. In faith we are able to see the God-possibilities in life.

Nothing is outside the scope and/or influence of our faith.

As we make the Kingdom of God our first priority and choice (Matthew 6:33), we will experience the greatest joys, as God shows up in every occasion, and we get to enjoy it. All needs and desires are met in His presence.

Faith yields to us the greater capacity of kingdom living.

It isn't about just getting by. God deals in the abundant. It is about the pleasure of God's heart. His heart does not have the boundaries or limits that we tend to place around ourselves. He has given us the faith to go beyond where the darkness led and go into an ever-expanding light and love.

From the beginning of anyone's walk with Christ, he or she is told to have faith. Salvation is "by faith." Anything that is needed in a believer's walk is "by faith." It takes an active faith to overcome, not a confusion of platitudes that sound of music but are in disharmony to the beating of the Father's heart.

The truth for many is that we have questioned ourselves out of our faith. All this confusion is because of a lack of knowledge and understanding of what faith is and what it is for. For many, there has been a paralysis of faith—no knowledge of how to live or how to activate faith in our lives.

Our attempt here is to dispel the confusion, not add to it, and to release and activate every believer into a life of the kingdom with all its benefits and blessings, no matter the cost. Yes, there is a cost for us; it is the surrender of our lives and will. For some, this may be too costly, but for others, it is a small price to pay in comparison to His payment to bring us to this point.

Faith is the answer and has the answer to so many things.

Yet many struggle to hold on to their faith when they should activate it and see all the Father is doing on their behalf. Faith is dangled in front of so many believers, but it eludes their grasp—but it is not a thing to hold. Faith in the common-church world is held up for comparison with others, yet there is frozen faith.

There is nothing to show for what has become faith today. The common church has even rewritten their dogmas and doctrines to fit the frozen faith that many have. We now accept things rather than having faith. This has been all in answer to a lack of understanding of what we should have: faith.

Faith the size of a mustard seed (Matthew 17:20) has become almost invisible. Many talk the talk but can't get off the couch to walk the walk. In the common church, true faith is no longer faith. It has been reduced to an untrue statement that isn't lived up to at all.

Faith has become the object of both worship and ridicule.

Some believer's faith is in their faith, instead of the focus being Christ of their faith.

Every single one of us needs to return to faith and to the time of our faith's first action: salvation. I am not saying to be immature but to remember how it first felt to exercise faith. This will restore the life of faith we started. Our repentance will guide us to turn from doubt to faith.

If we had faith at any time, it had to have been at the time of our being born again. If we did not exercise it then, then we are not born again. We have accepted a plan but have never truly believed. A believer has faith and lives by that faith.

The second death was pronounced before we even had life. There needs to be actual repentance in many churches, a return and turning back to the apostles' teaching. There needs to be a return to the Christ of our faith. If faith is the answer, then we need to live it.

Faith brings life and relationship. When has a statement of faith brought life? Maybe a statement of faith brought good feelings but not life.

The power of a statement is in the force behind it, not in the words. Our faith is that force.

When we see and hear from God, all things move from the realm of man and its impossibilities to the realm of the Kingdom of God, which is full of God-possibilities.

To define faith, a person might begin by quoting Hebrews 11:1 NASB, "Faith is the assurance of those things we have hoped for, and a strong conviction of those things we have yet to see." It is very poetic. Most would have to admit very little understanding, yet it would still be their definition of faith.

Yet this Scripture isn't a definition but more of a description of what takes place when faith is active. It is the introductory statement to the defining pictures of what faith truly is. It is a good place to start but not the place to end. It is but the first step to an adventure of kingdom proportions.

Many have called Hebrews 11 the "faith chapter." It is full of great escapades of faith. Whenever someone reads it, there is a rise of faith and awe from the recounting of past triumphs brought by faith. That reading is a convincing argument to us that it is "by faith" that all is done.

That whole chapter is about faith and those who have lived by faith. It is the "storybook definition" of faith. The reading of these accounts of active faith gives us the view we should have to understand and define it.

After any reading of Hebrews 11, we should notice that most Christians fall short of the full potential of their faith. These are stories of everyday people taking grasp of their faith and moving on it. It wasn't until after their activation of faith that they became more than they thought they were.

There are many who would say they live by faith, but in many of these cases, it is only a trust that they have put in themselves and not on or in God. It is simple to say, "I am living by faith" when everything is taken care of by our own initiatives and workings. This is not a bad thing in itself; but what about those things beyond us?

Yes, God did give us those gifts and talents in order to accomplish what we have, but is it by faith that these gifts and talents have worked the best. Have we shown the full potential of kingdom living?

"By faith" is trusting in God, not in our gifts or talents. This may sound confusing and almost like a game of semantics; but in whom do you trust and look for in all things? All things can direct our focus on Him, who is where all things begin; it's not about what we can do but about what He can do in and through us by faith and the Holy Spirit.

Reading Hebrews 11 should put us in the mind-set to live by faith. It leads us to go beyond what we are capable of doing ourselves. Each of the stories and characters show the accomplishment of things beyond the ordinary because of the more-than-ordinary God they served and who brought them through it. They tapped something within from God that produced incredible fruit. They are listed in Hebrews for our encouragement to live at a higher capacity than we have.

This is not just a place to cheer but the map of a life deeper than deep. In Hebrews 11, many have found definition, description, and example. But that has not made it easier for people to believe or receive. We can all readily agree it is by faith that we are to live, but when it comes to making it work in our own lives, many fall short.

Common-church practices have caused people to hesitate in stretching out, activating, or relying on their faith. Many have chosen to rely on the common church, which they see, rather than on God for things that God has provided through His act of salvation. Common-church Christians have a habit of ignoring the important things when it may require any concept toward selflessness.

The common belief is that this is for our standing or position. Common faith is for our own blessing and identity. It could be said that the measure of one's faith is based on what one has in comparison to everyone else. The common-church faith is tied into the level of participation in the workings and program of the organization.

In truth, we do not have faith for our benefit; it is for the benefit of the Father. He wants to share the blessings with us. He wants us to exercise the faith given so that He will have our companionship. We are granted open access and relationship with Him through our faith.

Our acts of faith are for Him; we get to have the adventure of our lives because of it.

As we continue to look at faith and what it is, we will find that it has less to do with us and more to do with Him, our Lord and Savior. There is no amount of working up the emotion of a thing that can make it happen. It is by Him and how He leads.

In living faith, we will see the greatest manifestation of faith and have the strongest grip on faith. As we embrace the life of faith, it will have a grip on us by the embrace of the Father. We will also have an understanding that will make it possible to not only do the things that Christ did but to help others do them also.

God gets pleasure from our acts of faith. He enjoys giving us the kingdom.

There appears to be a mystery to living by faith.

Individuals may have grasped a life of faith, yet communities do not do so. Faith is an absolute necessity to our lives, yet we do not have a grip on a proper use of faith or life of faith. Whether you want to call it being "led by the Spirit" or "walking in the Spirit," faith is the power behind that ability. Faith is the vision of stepping in the footsteps of Jesus as He leads us by the Holy Spirit.

We are fascinated with how others in our history have attained a great capacity of faith, but many haven't a clue on how to do it themselves. Again, we rewrite so much to make our mediocrity seem the highest level attainable. This shouldn't be in this age of such visitation and kingdom release.

That faith has a tendency to elude our grasp with any definition or absolute lends more to the mystery. We need constant encouragement to abandon ourselves to the cause of Christ. We need encouragement to allow our faith to arise so that a needy world can see and then believe.

It seems to be a constant labor to allowing ourselves to be gripped by God in such a way that we flow freely in the precinct of God's redemptive planning. Our constant struggle is keeping us in alignment with Him. This attempt to bring an open understanding of faith will be worth it if we get healed, saved, or even encouraged to try.

As He embraces us, the more He is seen on the throne of our lives and less of us in the battle of survival. He receives more glory to Himself as He embraces us with His love and the faith that He has granted to us.

There has to come to every person an understanding of faith at the capacity he or she is able to live by. Just as we each have different gifts, talents, and callings, we each have a faith capacity that may differ. Our faith may manifest itself differently, but it is all the faith of Christ.

God has measured out to us our faith (Romans 12:3). It activates every time we come into His presence, hear His voice, or read and hear His Word (Romans 10:17). Our faith will activate when we come into contact with a need that He wants met or at a place where He wants to manifest His love and power. He will lead us in the right paths, in order for us to manifest Him. These times are when others will come to know Him and experience His great love.

Faith is so important to our relationships with Him. It is imperative that our faith lives.

Our faith must be a growing faith, not a maintaining faith. Maintaining faith usually dies. Maintaining faith is inactive. When something goes inactive, it is dying or is dead (James 2:17). By the Holy Spirit, life returns to those who need it.

In the parable of the talents that Jesus told in Matthew 25, we see as much about faith as money in the telling. To hide away our faith is to displease the Master; to use and exercise it is to bring pleasure to the Master, which He pours out on those who show their faith and act upon it.

Our faith that has been given to us by God through the Holy Spirit spreads its life throughout all we do. A growing faith does more and greater works, just as Jesus did while on earth. There is no holding back with growing faith; it leads and brings new adventures for the believer each moment. The Father is active in His love for us. Our faith should be active in His love.

We are called to a higher and increasing capacity of faith. Those who are able to exceed their current capacity, for no other reason than believing, see awesome and unexplainable events and manifestations take place. It is at the highest capacity of faith that you and I are called to live. It is at that same capacity that we are to understand our faith (Romans 1:17; Galatians 3:9).

If we are to live by faith, then we need to gain an understanding of what that means as a word and as a lifestyle—a culture of the Kingdom of God. There must be an identification of what we are to have in order to hold on to it and be gripped by it.

We will be able to meet the opportunity of things in order to discern the proper steps to take in our lives to guarantee that we are living by faith and not by blurred sight. We need to capture the opportunity for faith, which brings the greatest pleasure to the Father.

Though with the things of God, there always seems to hang a mystery, yet all things are revealed through a deepening and maturing of our relationships with Him. The more we know Him, the more we seem to understand how to follow His ways.

There comes a change in that we become gripped instead of having a grip on faith.

There also comes those moments of surprise—those moments when God's presence drops in, and you must stop what you are doing and do something else. It all seems clear. The calling of God to act in faith becomes louder than any other voice. No explanation is needed, nor will any explanation fit.

It is one of those Gideon moments (Judges 6)—grinding grain one moment, and the next you are leading an army. Time and maturity do not get you ready for such things; only the call of God can qualify you. This is not a call or recommendation for immaturity but a call to grow in His grace, in order to be ready to say yes! Be ready and open to all that God may surprise you with.

Each of us may be called to live at a different capacity of faith, or it may require a different lifestyle. But it is our active faith in Him that brings him the greatest pleasure. We are not measured or compared to another's capacity but to what we have or have been destined for by His grace and peace toward us.

The individual who was given only one talent wasn't judged by how the individual with five or ten talents did. He was judged by what he didn't do. The Master didn't have them all report and then pronounce his decisions. As each one shared his fear or success, He gave each what He wanted that one to have, according to his obedience and faith.

One operated under fear of what he thought would happen. The other two operated under a desire to please the Master and give good testimony of His trust in them. One saw what was not there; the others saw what could be there.

At the minimum, we need to know the direction to go in order to fulfill His call. We may not have a full grasp of faith but we should know the correct direction and attitude through our relationships with Him. There should be enough of faith's grasp on us to get us going in the right direction.

FAITH: THE GOD-POSSIBLE

The Release of Faith

Questions still arise from Hebrews 11, which would be easily answered if this chapter truly contained the definition, along with the description and example. This chapter does give us an incredible amount of information concerning the unlimited usage and help that our activated faith can be.

The examples in this chapter set a high standard for the believer. Each example is a commitment to all or nothing before the Lord. These are incredible leaps of faith. There are those who suffered loss and great gains but were held in high account for their faith. Yet they did not count it loss but gain of the Father's pleasure.

The definition becomes clearer by the examples, but it does not have a *Webster's*-style definition written out. The stories give us principles and concepts to find and follow.

We need to know that these great feats of faith are circumstances of great pleasure for the Father that we can do—and do even more (2 Timothy 3:16–17).

There are those who tend to water down the stories of the Bible by explaining them as parables, myths, or legends. I can only assume that in this way they soothe some guilt for not operating at the capacity of faith to which they and the church are called.

A clearer indicator of the definition is found in Hebrews 12:1–2. This probably should have been included within the eleventh chapter. (Remember, the chapter and verse designations were added later to Scripture in order to make it easier to study and to identify readings.)

So read all forty-two verses as one thought and topic. Scripture interprets Scripture by comparing and melding together the wisdom it shares. We must be convinced in the truth of God's written Word in order to live to its and His expectations.

Noah: God spoke to Noah and told him to build a big boat for a flood that was coming. There had never been anything like this before. So God instructed him on what to do. He showed Noah the plan to save his family and the animals of the world. This process of hearing God, seeing the plans, and being obedient was counted as faith and a listing in the faith chapter.

Abraham: He was known as Abram at the time when he heard from God. God spoke to him and instructed him to leave his family and home. God's plan was to bring Abram to a new place to start generations of blessings and descendants. This process of hearing God and walking out God's plan was counted as faith; it was his first listing in the faith chapter.

Sarah: It was expected of the wife in that culture to have children, but Sarah was barren. When she recognized her inability to have children, she offered to Abraham her servant girl. But it was God's plan for her to have her own child, which He told her about on more than one occasion. When she accepted it, though, the promise was received. Her walking out the promise of God was counted as faith, and she was listed in the faith chapter.

Abraham: For some this may be a more significant act of faith than any other. After waiting many years for the promise of God to be fulfilled, God asked Abraham to give up the promise. It was time for a sacrifice, and Abraham was asked to give up his son. He chose to do it, knowing and believing that God would raise his son again. This process of hearing God and walking out God's plan was counted as faith.

Isaac: He saw the plan of God being worked out through his father. He wanted that imparted to his sons, Esau and Jacob. So he blessed them with continuing the plan. This process of hearing God and walking out God's plan was counted as faith and listed in the faith chapter.

Moses: He came to be known as the "Great Deliverer." From being saved from massacre to leading the Jews back to their home, from seeing God in the burning bush to all the instructions for the tabernacle, from parting the Red Sea to seeing the Promised Land from a mountaintop, Moses heard and saw the plan of God for the nation of Israel. This process of hearing God, seeing the plans, and being obedient was counted as faith and listed in the faith chapter.

Rahab, Gideon, Barak, Samson, Jephthah, David, Samuel, and more whose names we do not know are listed as people of faith. To God, these were incredible moments of faith that need to be inspirational to us. If you were to read their stories over again, you would find that they had a promise, a word, and a vision from God and stepped out in obedience to fulfill God's call on them.

There are things listed of great sacrifice, but it was all by faith.

Their names known and important to God gives us the idea of the importance of faith and how it involves Him and not us. Their names may not be listed because it was the obedience to their faith that was important, not their names. They had found that spot where they knew it was about Jesus.

Each one knew what God expected out of them—faith.

The results may not have always been clear, but their relationship with God gave them hope to trust in Him. The sacrifice that they may have made was not their focus. They gladly went where they were needed, without knowing the end, as long as it was what God wanted.

Faith has been proposed as being blind leaps into a great unknown—that in order to show our faith in God, we must step out into areas that appear risky. Though this existential thinking has truth in it, it does not give a true, complete picture of what faith is. You have the better visual as your faith is activated, for you see in the realms of all worlds and possibilities. The Kingdom of God is revealed by faith as we grow in our hope in Him, because of His great love, which He has freely shared with us.

Though we may not know the place of every step, we do know that the steps are placed for us by the Lord (Psalm 37:23). He leads us as we follow Him. As we will see, faith is based upon God's Word and Spirit. We know God is in control. With God in control, there is no leap of unknowing; it is only a leap into His hand.

There are times that the steps taken in faith seem blind to the casual observer, but to the one taking it, there is a leading that it is what has to be done. The outsider may not see the object of our faith, but the power broker of our faith knows exactly what is before us. We may be blind but our faith is not blind.

Our faith sees the unseen.

When a person is in a right relationship and fellowship with the Father, he or she knows to seek the leadings of the Father. The object becomes unimportant in comparison to pleasing the Father. It is not about where we are going but for whom we are going. It is not about the means or the ends but about pleasing Him.

This is what Hebrews 11:1 is about. Those times when a person acts in faith but not all the facts are known or seen is exactly what it is talking about. It is not the faith but what is happening when faith is drawn upon. You don't see the fulfillment of your faith in this reality until you have seen into the kingdom realm, but you know it will be there. Faith gives you the assurance that what He has promised, though not seen, will be active in your life.

You are assured of faith's existence, not because that is your faith but because of your faith. An active release of faith reveals the hand of God in your life.

Your faith draws on the hope of the need being met and the "other world" where the answer exists. Faith pulls two worlds together and erases the line between this reality and the greater reality of the Kingdom of God. A life of faith can be one that is recognized due to the leading of the Holy Spirit. We are led into a deeper relationship with Him as we walk in the steps of the Kingdom of God.

Because we are the "sons of God," we are given the favor and opportunity of being "led of the Spirit" (Romans 8:14 NASB). The Holy Spirit knows what is needed in our lives and what the destiny of our lives is. So He will draw us to the best place and position, in order for our faith to have the greatest connection to the provision of God for our lives and those around us.

God provides for us everything that is necessary.

This is a provision for every aspect of our lives. Many have equated provision only with the idea of finances. If our lives depended only on money, that would be all we would pursue, but life has more to it than that, such as peace and joy or even love. The list can go on.

There is no limit to the provision of God.

Provision is in all forms for what is needed for "life and godliness." God is there to provide for all needs, whether physical, spiritual, emotional, or any other level.

God sends to us through His Spirit, into our souls, the facts of what can be accomplished by our active faith. The Holy Spirit guides us to the place of action, when we rely on Him for all we need, do, or want. The strength of our relationships with Him will feed the capacity that we have for faith.

The Holy Spirit sees the past, present, and future. He sees the hidden places of all that is around and in us. He sees all around in space and time. Through His sight, we have the capacity of vision to exercise and activate our faith in order for the pleasure of God to be at its greatest capacity.

As a believer, we must learn and be confident of the voice of God. We should seek the ability to recognize the voice of God (John 10:1–5). With so many voices trying to get our attention, it will take discipline and concentration to filter out all but God's voice.

It is in the voice of God that our faith is nourished (Romans 10:17).

The children know their Father's voice and know He leads only in ways that are right. The direction is given when we listen for His voice (Isaiah 30:21).

The voice of God speaks to us of His love and care. It will be words of encouragement and comfort. His words lead to faith in Him, not in an institution. His words are not for packaging.

Some think that faith is our belief system, the "tenets of faith," or our doctrinal statement. The difficulty with that is that it deals with head knowledge and very little spirit. These are package deals that we can put in our pockets, but they have very little to do with the faith in Hebrews 11.

Most of the doctrines of the common church today are only bits of knowledge that separate that fellowship from other fellowships. There is no faith built up through this behavior.

There is more confidence in having correct theology than in the God of our theology. Because of our own shortcomings, we feel we need to give God an excuse for nothing happening. In reality, He needs no excuse. He needs an individual to rise to his or her full potential in faith.

There is no substitute for active faith.

We can know all there is to know and still not have a faith worth having. We must live by faith. Man tends to bring God down to his level, rather than his rising to God's. We need to learn the lessons of the Greeks and Romans, who fashioned their gods after themselves; the loss of faith caused them to lose all they had.

Knowledge is not evil, but any knowledge left alone leads to disaster. Knowledge will blind a person to put his confidence in what he knows, rather than trust what cannot be seen. Knowledge can be corrupted and misinterpreted. Knowledge is power, and power can corrupt.

To be of any benefit, knowledge must be brought under control with faith. There is no adventure until the two are combined. It would be better to have more faith than knowledge. I am not proposing ignorance of Christian doctrine. In the common-church world, the pattern has been that the higher the education is, the less we see the manifestations of faith. The more we know, the less we know Him.

Knowledge causes us to seek explanations rather than the pleasure of God. We want to explain things rather than just believe. The two, in proper use, can build the kingdom in such a way that many will come to seek the Lord of the kingdom. Signs and wonders will be the norm of a Christian life, instead of the rarity.

Faith needs to be understood to the capacity in which we are capable of believing. Knowledge freed by faith will allow us to see the miraculous in comparison to the mundane. Through faith we see the greatest reality of the Kingdom of God manifest into our simple reality.

Due what we know when God bursts on the scene in answer to our faith, it is not a surprise but a celebration. We recognize it and point it out for all to see and experience. Then the capacity of faith rises again. There are true signs and wonders that bring the awe of God into us for the celebration of His good pleasure.

Faith should never be overlooked. It is an important part of the believer's life. Hebrews 11:6 says that there is no way of pleasing God without faith. In this verse we not only see that faith is a prerequisite in our relationships with God, but the two words—faith and believe—are related. We have faith in God, and we believe in God. We show we have faith through our obedience but also by believing and trusting in Him for who He is. Our faith is more than knowing He is God but believing Jesus is God.

To believe in God is more than saying He exists; it is surrendering ourselves to Him and allowing our faith and belief in Him to guide us in all we do. Faith builds a relationship between us and God that brings us in submission to Him.

Faith requires us to seek and follow Him as though there is no separation between the two. We need to remain as close as possible. The strength of our relationships to Christ is important to the capacity of our faith.

Faith is our sight and vision of God.

In seeing Him, we live our lives, following His lead. There is a release and activation of God into situations when He contacts our faith, and then an amazing set of manifestations spring forth. Our faith brings to light all things needed for life and godliness.

You may ask, "Is it not enough for my salvation that I have faith?" Sure, if that is all you want, but Christ's death covers more than just our salvation. The act of salvation by Christ was more than "fire insurance."

There is a complete package involved with His death, burial, resurrection, and coming of the Holy Spirit. The package brought us wholeness—salvation, healing, and deliverance. Faith in Him gives us this package to live out and enjoy, bringing the highest pleasure to the Father.

A person's inactive faith makes it difficult to appropriate all that Christ bought for him or her through His death, burial, and resurrection. By exercising faith and by believing, we are now saved and made whole. We are also healed and freed from the past, any curse, and all power of sin. All believers need to appropriate all that Christ did for them by activating their faith in Him.

For many, faith is the hope and/or assurance that God has and/or will do what is needed. So they wait until that which is not seen becomes a reality. This is from their reading of Hebrews 11: 1—but this speaks of the evidence of our faith.

When we exercise our faith, there are miracles, hope, and assurance—a fruit of our faith. Hope is not faith, and neither is having assurance or confidence. Faith always produces a reaction and a fruit of itself. When we set our faith on Him for salvation, there was immediate fruit.

Faith is more of surrender than a reaching out. It is surrender to God's will and command. In surrendering, we put ourselves into the middle of His redemptive planning. There is no forcing the matter through confession or any kind of stance. It has everything to do with what God wants and has already set in order, as well as our ability to let it happen.

Faith is more than power but also the means to the power.

Exercising our faith does not allow us to tell God what to do or how to do things. We are His creation, not the other way around. Faith puts us in right standing in order for our obedience to make the greatest difference.

When was the last time you made God do anything? Is your faith stronger than God? Could this be more in line with why some things don't go your way? Could this be why some are not healed? Have you missed out because you are telling God what to do, rather than standing in faith and the authority given through it?

We can tell things and other beings what to do through our authority, but God will not be told what He has to do. That would eliminate Him as God. By definition, being God puts Him in charge.

But how many times have you heard God say, "I have a blessing for you. Just come to Me"? Our arrogance makes us think that what we do or have is important to the grand scheme of things. Our arrogance thinks that without us, God has nothing.

God has done more without us than with us. Does God need us, or does He want us to be such a part of Him and His plan that He wants to show pleasure toward us?

God *loves* us. He loved us in our sin. He *loves* us in our righteousness. Nothing changes His love for us. There is nothing that can separate us from that love (Romans 8:38–39).

He loves us unconditionally, deeply, and passionately. There is nothing that we can do that will make Him love us more. There is nothing that we can do that will make Him love us less.

Our faith doesn't change that fact, but it will change the circumstances and people around us. Because of the love of the Father, we seek ways to express this faith so that others will know Him. Our faith is about His love for us and others.

Our faith brings us closer to what He wishes us to be. We are made into the image that He originally planned for us at creation. We are made into His image. We will be like Him and as He intended, with our faith always at the ready.

Everything we have and have to do has to do with God. He gives our faith to us (Romans 12:3). He gave it to us to bring us into alignment with the purposes of God. In actuality, we stretch or activate our faith in answer to what the Father is calling us to do.

Our faith grips us into fulfilling the call of God. We would do well to reread the parable of the talents (Matthew 25:14–30) and search our hearts to see if we have invested our faith wisely.

The Scripture does say He will give us the desires of our hearts (Psalm 37:4). It is great to receive the desires of one's heart, but in this Scripture, the key is the first part, and that is our delight Him. To delight Him is to be pliable. He should be the true desire of our hearts.

The psalmist is saying that as we allow the Father to mold our hearts, it will be as His heart, so that even our desires are His, and we will have what we request. As we desire more of Him, and He becomes more of our desire, we will see the manifestation of His heart. We are not telling Him what we want; we are coming into alignment with what He wants for us, and we receive it.

This could be a hard concept in comparison to some teachings of faith. Some would have you believe that because you have "become a Christian," you automatically are sanctified—that you would never desire anything that is harmful, or that your proclamation is your level of faith, or that your checkbook shows your level of faith. Neither teaching fits Scripture, nor do they fit experience.

There are probably numerous more examples of what faith is not and any number of teachings that have twisted the use of faith. It has a lot to do with control. The more control a person wants, the more twisted the concept of faith. It may be hard to believe that this would happen in the church, but look at history and you will know the truth of it.

Just because a person says he is a Christian or has even recited a prayer of acceptance does not conclusively make him a believer and thus a friend of Jesus. Even a declaration of faith can be faked. We need to be aware of who is around us and of his fruit. There are more to words; we need to discern the motives and heart behind the words.

Confession of Christianity is not the same as a confession of faith in Christ.

Faith will produce a fruit that is recognizable as the hand of God moves, and faith will produce the results that the Father is seeking in each of our lives. By faith we will accomplish what is on His heart.

Faith is alive and will be known by its own life as it draws us to obedience in Christ. Our salvation, healing, and freedom are products of our active faith. Our faith will be duplicated in others as we share of our faith and its fruit.

Faith produces more faith.

I am not saying that works bring our salvation. I am saying that salvation is by faith; works will follow our faith as a fruit of our salvation but of our faith also. Works, by definition here, is doing what the Father has commanded or shown us. Works of faith can be non-active participation with the Father, just being in His presence.

Faith itself cannot be faked. You can have a false confidence but you cannot have false faith. There is false teaching, false doctrine, and false teeth, but those only affect your faith. There is no having false faith in God. You either have faith in God, or you don't. There is no middle-of-the-road faith.

You can fake having faith. You can fake your testimony of faith. You can fake being a person of faith, but you cannot fake your faith. Your fruit will bear out your faith. It will all show when the tests begin.

Our capacity of faith will be seen when we are faced with any test or trial or opportunity to show God. Whether it is a test of our character, or sickness, or simply being asked to pray for someone, we are going to see our faith manifested at the capacity we believe.

At times, the grace and mercy of God will stretch us beyond any perceived limits to get us to a new capacity. God wants to see us draw closer to Him. He wants us to have new experiences. He will stretch us to be closer to Him and fit us for the new experiences.

Many believers have more faith in their doctor than they have in God. Many will allow someone to pray for them, but in their minds they know they have a doctor's appointment, and if the prayer doesn't work to their satisfaction, they at least have the doctor. Giving God the last opportunity is not a sign of faith.

Going to the doctor takes more of a leap of faith, because we cannot be sure the doctor knows what is necessary. But God knows everything and will lead us in the right direction of prayer and authority. We have the faith that gives our authority its power.

The time taken to wait upon the Lord is less harmful than the drugs a person will take to ease the symptoms. Are doctors useless? No! But let us put them in the right position. It should be preventive. Doctors are practicing their knowledge; we live by faith. Doctors treat symptoms; God heals the whole person.

I am not saying, "Don't go to the doctor." I am saying to make sure your faith is real and placed in the right place.

Having faith does not make you perfect, but it helps in the making of you as a perfect being in Christ.

You can have accepted a false teaching of one kind or another and still have faith in God. You can make mistakes and still have faith. Your mistakes do not mean you can't or won't be used. The best example of that is Peter.

Peter was a disciple of Christ and a real handful for our Lord. We also see that there were many incredible things that took place in Peter's life because of the faith relationship he had with God.

In Peter's second epistle, he uses the statement, "to those who have received a faith of the same kind" (1:1 NASB). Would Peter have addressed that to us? Have we "received a faith of the same kind"? Here is a man who probably has been picked on more for his mistakes than his manifestation of faith.

Many like to concentrate on three events of Peter's life: 1) the time Jesus rebuked Peter when he opened his mouth carelessly; 2) his denial of Christ; 3) his walking on water and then sinking. Each of these expose Peter's shortcomings.

We like to point out the weak moments of a person in order to encourage ourselves that we can rise above our weaknesses. But have we risen as far as Peter in order to say we have "like precious faith"? Have we once again settled for mediocre thinking that the things of the Bible just don't happen anymore?

Peter attained a very high capacity of faith. Peter accomplished incredible feats of faith throughout his ministry—that should be our goal. Peter carried an anointing that allowed his faith to change many lives in miraculous ways. Here are some of the ways:

He walked on the water. Many point to the fact that he started to sink, but I am still amazed that he got out of the boat and walked on the water. The last time I got out of a boat in the middle of a body of water, I immediately sank. I have not heard of anyone who can walk on the water.

He healed the crippled man at the gate of the temple. He had nothing to give but the faith he had in Christ. Stretching out his faith, he brought healing to a man who had been crippled for a long time. I have seen some incredible healings in our services, but I believe that God wants greater ones.

He broke the barriers between the races. Paul may have been the apostle to the Gentiles, but it was Peter who built the bridge for him to cross. Even today, we see groups struggling to reconcile the races. But you can't reconcile what you are not willing to work beside or sit under their leadership.

His shadow would bring healing. He walked in such an incredible anointing and faith that people would lay the sick at the side of the road so that as Peter's shadow crossed them, they were healed. My shadow so far only brings relief from the sun.

Peter walked in faith. His weaknesses were no different from yours or mine. Yet he allowed what was in him to rise up and be bigger than himself, so that others could benefit.

In spite of weakness, he was able to allow the strength of God to push his faith beyond the limits of his weakness.

Our weaknesses become moments of His strength, as we allow more of Him to show in our lives and less of us. Here is what we need to do in order to see the manifestation of faith we are promised: allow God to push faith beyond the limits of our weaknesses (2 Corinthians 12:9).

It is a recurring theme—it is not about us but about the Holy Spirit of the Father, working through us. We can stand in faith, based on the word of the Father.

We are destined and called to do greater works than Jesus did. We can obtain "like precious faith," We have it already; we just need to exercise it and find opportunity to stretch it out.

We may not have done all that Peter did, but we are destined to those great works. We are a part of the family of faith and need to follow the patterns set before us to accomplish the things upon the heart of the Father. As the Father's love takes us in hand, we must grip our destiny as we grip our faith and see a world changed.

By faith, the great saints of the Old Testament accomplished mighty feats of faith, and they were looking forward to Christ. The New Testament is full of exploits of faith, done by both our Savior and the disciples. It is no wonder the Father showed such pleasure in His Son.

Faith pleases the Father, and faith accomplishes the will of the Father.

Faith is more than a power and more than a belief. Faith is more than a proclamation. Faith is a way of life and a pattern, both of our thinking and of our walk with Christ.

Faith is a major key to a Christian life.

The only way for Hebrews 11:1 to make sense as a definition of Faith is if we put it with Hebrews 12:1–2. The only way we can hope is to have something in our sight. Hebrews 12:1–2 (author's paraphrase) says, "Envision Jesus." There must be some concept of a thing in order for it to be hoped for.

We are clearly told here to see Jesus—see what He is doing and saying. He is modeling for us what is pleasing to the Father. He is showing us how our faith will be completed. Here is hope seeing Him.

There must be evidence of a thing before you can hope for it.

The problem with just hoping is that there is no guarantee of its actually happening. Faith is more than hope. In faith, a thing will happen, because it has been seen and done through our faith. Faith is the guarantee of those things that are hoped for.

A person of faith has seen the thing and thus hopes and believes until it comes about.

Faith, hope, and love all combine to bring the Kingdom of God in incredible manifestation.

Sometimes, because of what we know about God, we trim down our faith. We tend to exchange knowing about a person for having a relationship with them. It is difficult to have faith in someone when there is no real relationship with that person.

We know He can, but do we know that He *will?* Because we know that He is so great, we wonder if we are important enough to catch His attention. The scenario continues in a circle. But He wants to bless us, He can bless us, and He is blessing us.

The usefulness of our knowledge is based on the depth of the relationship. We only know in part. Because we have only achieved a certain level in our relationships with God, we have only a minute level of knowledge.

The deeper we go in our relationships with Him, the more we know of Him and the more we can act out of faith. The knowledge will be of Him and not of just facts about Him.

When this happens, we are acting out of relationship and not knowledge. Our knowledge will convince us that it can't happen. But our relationships with the Father will convince us it *can* happen. It will convince us that He has already begun the work.

Being close to the Father will allow us to hear His heartbeat, and we will see what has been accomplished through faith and what is yet to be accomplished. There is no doubt, so we will have no doubt within ourselves to see all the Father wants to bless us with.

The love of the Father is deep and wide (Ephesians 3:17–19). It is within our knowing. If there is nothing that can separate us from the love of God (Romans 8:38–39), then we need to recognize the power of that love. Our relationships are based on and in that love. The closer we are to the heart of God, the more we become engulfed in His love.

Our faith becomes as limitless as His love. This brings to us an opportunity for endless adventure.

Faith isn't stepping into the unknown. All things are known through His love. Faith steps into the reality of God. There is no unknown with Him. When we exercise what He has given us, it is a step with Him, and He sees the beginning and the end.

That is what faith is all about—*He knows.*

It does not matter if things look impossible to us or that the resources do not seem to be there. Our faith is established upon the matter of a different world. As in the beginning, God speaks a word, and from nothing, all is created. As sons of God, we live by the principles of the Kingdom of God. In that kingdom, there are only possibilities, and resources are unlimited.

Some wait to fulfill the call until everything is organized. Some will step out, having heard the call with anticipation of the answers as they go. Either way is correct, as long as it is the way God has called us to do it.

We get caught up in method at times, when all we need to be is caught up in Him. We think it has to do with how we hold our hands, whether heat or cold is generated from our hands, or oil is dripping from our hands—all of this is nothing to faith. If we are caught up with Him, we have everything at our disposal that is needed for "life and godliness."

Our faith is stretched into action when we hear God speak. God speaks only what He wants done. This is what separates faith from wishful thinking, hope, or even positive thinking. Faith is established by what God speaks.

We do not create from nothing, but His Word causes all things to be. Out of obedience to what He says, our faith connects with the living Word to manifest the power of God through miracles, signs and wonders, and healings. Faith, obedience, and God's Word is all that is needed in order for the presence of God to be manifested in our lives.

Faith is the authority to see that what He has said will come to pass. The things that will be called into being are spoken first by the Father, and then we agree with Him for the fulfillment on our behalf and for His pleasure.

Matthew 21:18–22 tells us that Jesus was very emphatic that we were to "have faith in God!" He was letting us know that our active faith allows us to change nature (moving mountains) and that we could ask anything and receive it. These are things that are ours by relationship and position in the Kingdom of God.

The standard of life in the kingdom is based on our faith (Romans 1:17). We are warned against doubt and unbelief. He didn't rebuke the disciples for not having faith but for allowing their faith to be "little." To have little faith is to allow your faith to lack the focus and activation to make the things happen as they should.

It is with faith that we please God (Hebrews 11:6). The greatest enjoyment that we can have within the kingdom is bringing pleasure to God our Father. In the Kingdom of God, all things are done for the glory and pleasure of the King. By faith, we accomplish the things that Jesus did and that we were to also do. Our obedience to the Father pleases Him. As with any Father, a child's obedience brings pleasure and pride to the heart.

When we do not stand in what God has said for us to stand in, we are not in obedience or alignment to His Word. We shrink our faith when we do not stand in who we are in Christ. By not taking up our authority in Him, we allow our faith to become little. The following is some of what we should know of who we are:

1. We are of the "household of faith" (Galatians 6:10 NASB).
2. We are His friend (John 15:15).
3. We are God's children (Romans 8:16).
4. We are heirs with Christ (Romans 8:17).
5. We are the body of Christ (1 Corinthians 6:15).

6. We are the Dwelling Place of God - I Corinthians 6:19).
7. We are chosen (Romans 11:5–7).
8. We are the righteousness of Christ (Romans 4:1–9).
9. We are royal kings and priests (1 Peter 2:9).
10. We are loved (John 3:16).

We are here for His good pleasure. He has given to us everything we need that "pertains to life and godliness" (2 Peter 1:3 NASB). This is by the faith given to us by God (Romans 12:3). Our faith is not the list of what we believe in; it is our alignment with whom we believe. Faith is our active obedience to what we see the Father do and what we hear the Father say.

We must have faith, but if we do not know what faith is, we do not know how to wield our faith. Faith reveals the depth of our relationships with Him. There are certain things that we should know in the pursuit of being the most effective in our faith:

First, we need to know that our faith was given to us (Romans 12:1–3). This is important to know and understand because we have to keep the focus on Him. Too much emphasis has been placed on what we can do or accomplish. We have defined works as what has to do with our abilities, when it really has to do with what God is doing. He makes us able to do what He has called us to do. He hasn't chosen us according to our own abilities.

We are to put ourselves into the right position of who we are in Christ. We are not to think of ourselves outside of who we are in Christ. He gave us the faith so that we can have the right thinking so to enjoy the things that are "good and acceptable and perfect" (Romans 12:2 NASB). God has made everything possible for us to live at the highest capacity of our faith. He has not short-changed us in any area of life.

Second, our faith is for a purpose. We show evidence of faith in who we are and what we may do. Faith is not a verbal gift; it is a power gift. Just to say you have faith will not be enough to fulfill God's plan. Our faith must be vital and alive. We do the things that we see the Father do and those things that we hear Him say to do (John 8:28–29; James 2:14–17; John 15:13–14; Romans 12:4–8). Keeping our eyes on Jesus and our ears open to His voice gives us the opportunity to walk out the purposes of God.

Third, there is no limit to what our faith can accomplish for God. Is there anything too hard for God? There is a difference in what God doesn't want to do and what He can't do. The only limitation that can happen to faith is the capacity for doubt that we may manifest. There is to be a total abandonment to God's boundless love for us. Eighteenth-century theologian Jonathan Edwards once said, "We should not limit God where He has not limited Himself."

We read the stories of Jesus in the Bible, and we think that is nice. We may even think it might be nice to do some of what He did, even though we are promised to do even more and greater things. There is only one thing that stands in our way of these things—it is *us*, not our faith but in how we activate it; not God's ability but our view of God.

Fourth, faith will protect us from the schemes and weapons of the enemy. We hold up our faith as a shield. The protection is for our whole bodies so that we can be about the Father's business (Ephesians 6:16; Isaiah 54:17; Act 3:16).

We are coming into a better understanding of our faith as we walk with Him. The more we see Him at work in each of our lives, the greater our exercise of faith. We are learning to see and recognize the voice and actions of God. We are not blind to how God looks. We have over-excused ourselves because of the times we closed our eyes to what He was about.

God has never failed. We have only failed ourselves while convincing ourselves that it was someone else's fault. It is time to take up what He has given us and live in the blessing and inheritance we have. It is our responsibility to trust in Him, so that we will be aligned with His purposes. Through the events of the cross to Pentecost, Jesus erased the failures and began remake us into the image that He had intended us to be in.

This is important, because every one of us, at one time or another, has questioned our own faith. We have questioned our position in Christ. We have questioned the why's of our lives. We have logged every prayer that wasn't answered immediately in our brains and have blamed ourselves. We have equated it to our possibly not being saved, not having God's attention or favor, or not doing anything correct.

We have to rely on our faith and the "Creator and Completer" of our faith. We question our faith because we listen to lies. If we would understand faith, we would know that it isn't about us but about Him. Through acknowledging Him and being obedient to His actions and words, we rise to the capacity of His love.

Our faith, when it is active, drowns out the lies and enhances the grace of God.

Our faith gives us the empowerment to build into our relationships with the Father. It exposes the falsehoods and illumines the place of His presence. It highlights the heartbeat of the Father. Our faith brings us into alignment with the will and Holy Spirit of God. Our faith then causes us to fulfill the plans within the heart of God. Jesus told us to have faith. He didn't complicate things; we have done that. He wants us free.

There are reasons that God speaks in several places of the Light. In the Light we see all that is there. Light exposes the plots and tricks of the enemy. The Light brings focus to what the Father is doing, allowing us to follow Him and keep in step with Him. The Light brings attention to what the Father is doing. It helps us to remember that it is about Him. The exposure of Him is the releasing of love.

This is our faith; we see and hear God. We do only what He says and does. We do not look to see what will benefit us but what brings glory to Him. We do not concern ourselves with our shortcomings or mistakes. Our lives are not our own. We have been bought with a price. We are people of faith.

Our faith is our active obedience to what we see the Father doing and what we hear Him saying to be done.

We should not accept the lie that we can't, neither should be accept the lie that we are anything less than that which we have been declared. We are children of God, part of the household of faith, and an heir and joint heir with Christ. By faith, we can do all things through Christ. By faith, we can move mountains. Our faith grows large as we see the Father, and He sees us.

HOPE: THE GOD-PERSPECTIVE

When it turns dark at the end of the day, you turn on a light. But what happens when you can't find the light switch? Similarly, which way do you turn when you can't see which way you are facing? How real do the hidden dangers in the darkness become your concern and focus?

In these moments, the darkness takes on a tangible feel. It almost has texture. It all seems real. The darkness lends itself to things that you would not normally think and that will cause you to miss that which you need the most. Darkness, though it can be deceptive and dangerous, can be turned positive by driving us to the Light.

While in the dark, you reach out to grab for something that will help, but many times it seems as though nothing is there, or it slips from your fingers. If you do grab something, how sure can you be that it is what is needed? What are your options? You can give up, panic, and allow despair to take over, or you can keep searching until you find the switch, shout for help, deny the darkness, or use a match. No matter the feeling or emotion, you want something more—you want something to happen.

You go from wishing that something would happen to hoping beyond hope that the situation will change. You want something to happen; you hope it will happen now. Hope is a large part of the power that keeps us going, enabling us to make it through any situation.

Hope becomes an important part of the driving force for a good quality of life.

No matter what you choose for your life experience, few would choose to remain in darkness if they could avoid it. They want to be in the light. Even as adults, we can remember the childhood fears of what our imaginations told us was hidden in the darkness, making those things more real than imaginary.

Darkness can become the embodiment of our fears, even though most of our fears are not based on any type of reality. The noise of things not there or the breezes through unopened windows make the presence of darkness more tangible, and it stirs the fears to higher frustrations and paranoia. A decision gets made to somehow try to dispel the darkness—to overcome it.

Most do not want to lose themselves in the darkness; to become a part of it; forgotten and avoided. Most of us do not want the fear within our imaginations to become the realities of our present. In our lack of hope, we will build what we thought would be a fortress to protect us, but it ends up being a prison. The bricks of our fears never lay a straight or level foundation; they build more obstacles and become stumbling blocks in life.

We need to avoid decision making while in a state of panic. We should make a conscious, heartfelt, and clear-thinking adjustment to go after the light and take only the help that God offers to us. God, our Father, knows what we need and how to make everything turn to our benefit (Romans 8:26–28). He is more than the object of our hope.

Hope can bring the light to our paths so that the stumbling blocks become the stepping-stones to our destiny.

As long as you keep going and keep pursuing life, hope will lead to faith and love, but when you stop. Hope seems to fade and go away. When you trip and fall, the risk is in not getting up and failing to reach the goal. But you must get up; you must take another step; you must push on. For some, to keep pushing through until the answer comes is simple; for others, there is always a battle. But hope will lift you by its strength to reach a higher and better place in life.

For some, certain times seem to attack any hope they think they have. The constant beating to cause hopelessness blocks the fact that the hope we need is always there for us. We can grip tighter to this hope. Hope is never far away.

Though the darkness would have us believe that hope is not there, hope is always with us.

We hold to hope to keep us from falling further toward despair and darkness. This is part of the deception of the darkness—that hope is not there. It can be easy to believe there is no hope when we are exhausting ourselves, battling what we cannot see, battling lies that seem so true. That is the only power darkness can use over us—the power of deception. Darkness cannot overcome hope, but it can try to deceive us into believing it can.

We must learn to discern the truth. The truth brings freedom when we follow it and believe it.

A person who loses his grip on hope risks losing to the darkness and despair. The risk is in never making it out. A journey that seems to take forever causes one to lose concept of the goal—the goal of being with the Father and being changed into the image He originally intended. The loss of one's grip is equal to losing everything; life seemingly slips away, the more one thinks he is slipping from hope.

The lifeline of hope that some have held onto so tightly slips through their grip, and all their feelings and emotions get out of control, telling them they are lost. They do not know where they are going. There is a loss of purpose and direction when there is a loss of relationship with hope. Many will forget to move, for fear of what might happen to them. The lack of hope can be paralyzing.

Even the perception that we have lost hope can be harmful, because that is not a fact based on truth but lies and deception. Hope is a bigger part of life than what many will admit. Hope empowers us to face the paths of our lives, as faith gives us the ability to walk in His ways.

Hope is an incredible power.

The power of hope helps us in our abilities to see and reach out for our destiny and goals of life. Hope is bound to faith in order for us to fulfill the call of God in our lives. If faith is necessary to please God (Hebrews 11:6), then hope will get us to the path of the life of faith. In our faith, we are in obedience to what we see and hear from the Father. His great pleasure poured over us will embolden us with hope. This hope keeps us on the path of all God-possibilities.

Hope becomes a motivator to see all that God has laid out for us. We need to encourage ourselves to hold tight to the hope that is important to our lives and destiny. Darkness will tell us we are lost and hopeless, but the truth is, we are in the hand of God and are victorious in Him. The darkness would have us fail because of what we may not see, but hope knows better because of who we know.

We have to protect this hope and our relationships to it.

Though hope will never fail us or leave us, at times we think and feel we are no longer connected. In those times, hope may present itself in unseen and intangible ways, but hope is always there. It is imperative that we do all we can to maintain hope, even in times where we do not see a reason to hope.

We need hope the most in those times when circumstances seem the worst.

Hope illuminates the path that directs our faith to get us through any situation and all circumstances. It is that powerful and that necessary. Though we may be surrounded by contrary evidence, the truth is that hope is there to see us through to the activation of our faith. When our faith is active and has been released, it is our hope that drives us to the strength of our faith, which causes the fulfillment of our destinies.

A person can learn to be content in the darkness, but generally, no one chooses to be subjected to complete darkness. Nor do many choose to be lost or in a state of complete despair, confusion, and helplessness. A healthy person will not choose a path that would lead to loss; pain, or any inability to be whole.

A believer's wholeness need not be sacrificed for any reason. It is not a price we need to pay. This is the price Jesus already paid for everyone in the events of the cross to Pentecost. There is no need to be under any negative effects of the darkness. We are made to live in light and to reflect the light of truth and wholeness that the Father made us in.

The despair, fear, and anxiety that accompany the experiences of darkness cultivate a sense of hopelessness. A person in this circumstance begins to feel as though he should not have tried or that he was never meant for more than what he has become. It is as though hopelessness has drained him of any desire, motivation, or ability to get out of where he is. He begins to feel as though there is no need to do anything to change the situation; he is not convinced that it will make any difference. There is no hope.

Faith is blocked; the connection to it is lost. There is no fulfillment of our calls and destinies. We can't see the answer because of looking downward. In these times, we are not sure of our hope; neither are we sure of life.

Being without hope is just a step away from death.

No one wants to experience a premature death; hopelessness is not on anyone's "bucket list." Real living is not about facing death; it is about fulfilling hope's dreams. Our lives are about fulfilling the calls and destinies of our lives. Living is about taking our destinies in hand and fulfilling calls that are more than ourselves.

Hope is about rising above the level of commonness to the level of creation that God intended when He created us in His image and likeness (Genesis 1:27; 1 John 3:2). His hope in us grows out of what He created in us. His hope in us is eternal. We need to find that place where we have an equal grasp on our hope and that same grasp has us. There is a place where we are enveloped in His light and grasped by His love.

Hope never fails or weakens with Him.

To make it through times of darkness and the challenges of life, we need to keep our minds in focus. It is a discipline to keep focused on Him and the answer of life. A steadfast mind finds peace (Isaiah 26:3). If we think failure, we will fail. That is when the darkness begins to fill in the space of retreating light—the light fades and retreats when thinking loses its focus.

Before the darkness takes root, hope needs to grab the mind so that the soul does not despair but pursues the light of truth for our lives. The peace of God that envelops us will strengthen us to be able to hold onto the hope we have. It is to our benefit to wrap ourselves in the hope that brings us to know that we have the faith to make it through and the love that will comfort and protect us. In these three, we are more than conquerors (Romans 8:37).

It is not our faith that keeps us going; it is our hope. Our faith gets us out of any situation from which we need to be delivered. Faith manifests what hope can know. It is hope that empowers us to take another step. Hope steadies us, so that our faith helps us take the next step. Faith is a "now power," whereas hope always points to the future.

Hope will keep us moving to the bright future as faith establishes the steps that we take.

Faith is an assurance of the heart and soul, whereas hope is the mind-set. Hope energizes us to activate our faith into any situation, no matter what it may be, so that we walk in life and victory. When we stand in hope, we stand straighter and taller, above the circumstance. We can know the Father, and our faith reacts because hope held us up high, above the darkness.

Hope can raise us up to a place where we know that we cannot be stopped. Hope can be measured and influenced by the pattern of our thinking. Our souls can seemingly be lost by the wrong thinking or mind-set. A state of confusion or loss can keep us distracted from the goal before us.

If we can't think it or focus on it, we can't activate the faith needed to overcome, build, or participate in the God-possibilities.

This will lead to great feelings of despair and loss. Spiritual loss can be more hurtful and devastating than physical loss. Losing hope can paralyze us and keep us from reaching out for help and salvation. Faith will not be activated. In a state of hopelessness, we cannot move forward. In fact, we do not move, because we do not know which way to turn for the help we have become desperate for.

Our faith is not activated in hopelessness; it is blocked from fulfilling the destiny and call in our lives. When we cannot activate our faith, we do not receive the fullness of all God has for us. We cannot receive when we cannot hope. When we are unable to activate faith, we are at our lowest in hope. It becomes very important to pay close attention to every aspect of our lives to make sure we are where we should be and are in good health in all areas.

There is a very strong relationship between hope and faith. Our use of hope and faith is in direct relation with our thinking. Our thinking reveals who and what we are (Proverbs 23:7). Our hope is based and founded in what and who we know and think.

We must think in terms of what He thinks (Philippians 2:5; Colossians 3:2). Our thinking is what can define us and give us direction for our lives (Proverbs 23:7; Philippians 4:6–7).

Our thinking will define our direction and our being.

Our uncontrolled and undisciplined thoughts can drive us further into darkness and despair. The lack of control and focus can cause us to freeze and lose direction and especially hope. We must keep our minds in the path of God and not the world (Romans 12:1–2). Our thinking can drive our way through to hope as we realize that there is always a way through.

Proper thinking can spark the light of hope so that we can watch our faith form the answer to our situation.

We see the answer and workings of God, and we know that our hope was not in vain and our faith is real. Our thinking can raise or drown the perception of our hope. It is important for us to think on the right things (Philippians 4:8).

It is in our thinking that the blessings of life can be most manifested.

Many events begin as a thought and then grow into a tragedy or a victory, depending on what we do with our thinking. Our thinking can entrap and drain our hope of its power to build faith. Our thoughts empower the hope and faith within, to hold tight to what God is doing in us and for us. Our thoughts can help us draw ourselves into the fulfillment of God's call. Our thoughts are controlled and fed by what we put into our brains. It is very important that we put in things that are good, uplifting, and even entertaining.

The exercise of our minds is as important as the exercise of our bodies.

Just as some food is more nutritional than other food to keep our bodies strong and healthy, there are such things for the mind. There is also a relationship between the health of the body and the health of the mind. When we feel good physically, it is easier to think right. When we think right, we will take better care of our bodies. When all things in our lives are well, we are whole and then can better live the life of the kingdom of God. We feed ourselves to maintain the wholeness, not to necessarily make us whole.

A lot of material had been produced to mold the mind-set of people. Some are searching for greater answers and a higher way of life. Some are just looking to take the next step and to get out of the situation they are in. They are not looking for the long term but the immediate relief of their circumstance. A feeling of relief becomes more important than what truth may be. When a person is wrestling with despair and hopelessness, immediate relief is all that seems to matter, without any concern for what is next.

People may sacrifice the long term for the immediate. We do not always think things through when we are struggling. In those times that we feel we have lost hope, we reach for anything that will help or bring some relief, without thinking through the consequences. Relief doesn't always mean we have been helped or have won our salvation.

Some items do make a person feel good about themselves for a time, but if they do not remain completely focused on the path to their utopia, things may become dark and confusing. Many times people become distracted by the next and newest plan, which can add to the lack of hope. As we have seen an increase in those going into the studies of counseling, psychiatry, psychology, and such, we must realize that a battle for the mind is taking place.

We see these increases in the common church as well as in the non-believing world. Advertising and marketing are in a battle for your thinking. Many of the ministry, Bible schools, and colleges are training more counselors than they are pastors. There is a battle for the mind and emotions of people, but the answer is not in psychology. The use of the tools within psychology may clarify some points and issues of your life; it may help you gain a new focus, but permanent fixes of life is in Him.

Our only hope is in Christ and His Word.

Preaching (in many cases) is no longer the "declaration of the good news"; it has become a lecture or motivational speech to feeling better. The encouragement is to think positive rather than have faith and hope in God. Thinking positive is not a bad thing in itself, but it falls short of where we should be as believers. Though many sermons can take such a tone, it is not about making people feel better but giving them opportunity and help to be better. With all this going on in a person's life, the grasp of hope can easily slip.

Our minds can be brought into focus of the hope we are to have in Christ. It is more than thinking right. Our thoughts and hope need to lead us to see and walk right. In this way, we will know the foundation on which we stand. Hope lets us know in whom we believe and on whom we can rely. All things about who we are and the relationships we have are based on Jesus.

He is the Creator and completer of the work that is going on within us (Hebrews 12:1–2; Philippians 1:6). He is the target of our focus. He is the standard by which we can measure the strength of our hope. Though there are times that life seems to be a storm or even a war, hope can still be strong, giving way to peace.

In hope, it isn't the storm that we focus on; it is on the knowledge that He is with us. As long as we know Him and walk in Him, our hope will raise us higher than any storm or difficulty that may come our way. Hope brings us to a new experience of life, which reminds us of how things were intended. God originally intended for us to always recognize the hope that lives in every believer. He wants us to know the strength of our hope and how He carries us in life.

Our hope will carry us through anything that life can bring our way.

It is important for us as believers to remain focused on our true hope, who is Jesus Christ (Colossians 1:27; 1 Timothy 1:1). The level of focus and the strength of our hope can be measured by our relationships with Him. When it is said that "Jesus is the answer," it is literally referring to Jesus as our hope, author of faith and love, who will carry us through any circumstance. He will keep us safe during all situations and circumstances.

It is not a flippant answer to say, "Turn to Jesus." It is the focus of the truth and our hope that gives us the overcomer mentality and victorious lifestyle. Our hope makes our foundations strong and our steps steady. It is in hope that we build and welcome the atmosphere of faith in which we live the Christ-like life that we have been called to walk in.

Our real hope is in becoming more like Jesus (1 John 3:2–3), not in blending into the crowd of blandness. The common church is guilty of slipping into what fits the immediate, into what is easy, by trying to appease the world instead of changing the world. We are called to make disciples, not bulk up our church memberships. Numbers only represent a small measurement of how discipleship is progressing. Hope isn't about quantity but quality of the disciples.

The thinking is that if we are accepted, we will be listened to, but why should anyone change when we do not offer any difference? When we are dealing with the same problems and situations within the common church as in the world, with little progress and little change of life, why follow Christ? There is no difference in the results. Though life with Christ is simple, it isn't necessarily easy. There are those who want everything given to them without living up to the standard of hope that Christ offers and exemplifies to us.

The common church teaches us to think positively, rather than to think right, which is the strongest of positive thoughts. We are called to personify the person who has called us to be His representative. Our lives are to follow the example and pattern laid out for us by Jesus. We are called to have hope and to represent the hope that is needed in a world in battle for peace of mind.

The hope we are given is in contrast to the confusion and despair that the world and the enemy try to force upon everyone. We give our hope to others as freely as hope came to us (1 Peter 3:15). This is fulfilling the command of Jesus to "go into the world and make disciples" (Matthew 28:18–20, author's paraphrase). In this work, we are building ourselves and others in faith and hope.

As believers, we are children of God and should know the family expectations—to live life to its fullest and within the inheritance we are given. Our lives should be in sharp contrast to the way of the world, causing the world to question us (1 Peter 3:15). In times when darkness tries to press in around us, our hope should shine in order to bring others to the faith that God freely provides. There should be a difference in our lives, in contrast to how unbelievers live.

Our salvation is more than a ticket to heaven.

The hope we hold should be evident in all we do. It is more than having a plan; our hope is the very Light that illumines our paths. God has predestined us to things that go beyond our imaginations (Romans 8:29–30; Isaiah 55:9; Ephesians 1:5–12). We walk in hope that is within the steps of God and His love (Psalm 37:23). In hope, we know that God is taking care of all things that have to do with our lives.

We know the promises of God are for us, and they are true (2 Corinthians 1:20). The facts that we may see do not always measure up to the truth that we know. It is the truth that we know that provides our freedom, not the circumstances we see or any supposed fact that presents itself. Hope brings us to the knowledge of who He is and the truth of what His Word has said for our lives.

The immediate is not always the final answer.

When there is no progress in our lives and no growth or maturity, we soon see that death will follow. When we are not on the right path for life, we slide back into practices that do not promote hope; they do not encourage life. It is a process of dying.

In death, there is no hope. We must grasp hope and know Him to guide us to the point of faith needed to fulfill all destinies in our lives. Hope builds us up and builds into us. We are being built into His image to give the world of non-believers the opportunity to know Him as He wants to be known. Our hope is in His promise to be with us and to fulfill His Word in our lives.

The way of God is full of life, growth, and opportunity.

Our hope in Him guides us through the paths of life that provide the greatest opportunity for growth, maturity, and faith. The light of our hope not only keeps the darkness and despair away, but it also guides our steps in the path of God. It is like a shepherd who takes proper care of his sheep; he protects, feeds, and cares for each one. None of the sheep under the care of a good shepherd ever worries; it knows it is being watched and cared for (Psalm 23). We know He is all that He says, and He will do as He says.

There is great benefit to taking notice of this special gift and foundational power of our lives. The benefits are not for just us but for all those who are around us, especially to God, who receives all the praise and glory for what He does. He does things well. We are at our best when we establish ourselves upon those things that last and not on those things that fade and die.

Our lives and relationships with Him are with an ageless God, who is from everlasting to everlasting (Psalm 90:2). He does not fail (Lamentations 3:21–24). Hope is one of three gifts and powers that remain when all else may fail (1 Corinthians 13:13). We can trust in Him and know that we will be led through any circumstance or situation.

There is always a way of escape (1 Corinthians 10:13). We have a hope that is strong, steadfast, and sure. The desire and hope that has been freely given will always be there for us. We know that all blessings are ready to be poured out on us. We know He is able to do more than we can imagine or think (Ephesians 3:20–21). He goes beyond what we can think and know.

There are things that come into our lives that seem to be stable and strong, but they are not necessarily long lasting. We are not building for the moment but for eternity. But the hope that is a part of every believer's life remains true and strong, making the difference for our faith and love to keep us in the right paths.

Hope remains active in our lives, so that we will see the completion of the work that was begun in us by Christ (Philippians 1:6). We will be made like Him, impacting lives around us, being victorious in Him. Our hope can be contagious, allowing others to see Jesus for who He truly is and to get to know Him as He wants to be known. He wants us to know Him in His power (Philippians 3:8–11). He remains faithful; He never changes; He remains our hope. He wants us to know Him in all that He is. Knowing Him is more than just knowing facts about Him.

Knowing Him is to know Him as He wants to be known, in all His Love.

The Father's greatest gift to us has been the revelation of Him in Spirit and in flesh. He has not hidden anything from those who seek and pursue Him. It may take time and lessons to understand the revelations to which we are exposed. Each event and revelation should lead us to a place and position in hope. They lead to a better relationship with Him.

Jesus continually looks for ways to grab our attention to show us Himself in all His glory.

When we can capture any vision and revelation of Him, our hope is strengthened and stabilized. Our hope is at its strongest in our lives as we move from just knowing to also seeing. With hope active in our lives, His faith and love is revealed and can be activated to bring greater glory to the Father. Hope does more than make us feel better; it gives us knowledge of a better person than what we were. We are no longer the wretched man we were because of the grace of God that is freely shared with us.

Hope will reveal to us the work that is being done in and through us, by Jesus through the Holy Spirit (Philippians 1:6; Jeremiah 18:6). Hope is more than wishful thinking or a good feeling about something. Hope gives us that assurance that "we know, that we know, that we know." We are made more into His image each day (1 John 3:2). The more of His image in us that we see and capture, the more we will walk in the strength and anointing of the Holy Spirit.

We can rest in this hope of His work until He appears again at what many call the second coming (Titus 2:13). Every appearance, revelation, and manifestation of Him has more of an impact on the image that was originally intended to show in us. The work being done in us is not to just make us better; it is to make us to be like Him.

We are His representative and have the opportunity to show why we have hope. We must take the opportunity to set a new standard of living that is set in freedom, not in bondage that leads to darkness. Hope is the lamp stand on the paths of life, for He is the "Light of the world" (John 9:5 NASB). We gain hope by His Word guiding us to Him (Psalm 119:105).

We have hope because we know He will lead us in the right paths.

The hope within us guides us through the maturation process to becoming more like Him. The more we are like Him, the more we rise to the capacity of faith and love that we have been called to. That capacity of faith and love that is built in us will get us through this adventure of life and will help us to understand and know Him as He wants to be known. What we know and who we know is built into the capacity in which we are able to share with others.

We can reach a height of maturity that leaves no question of who we belong to and who we have a relationship with. The work done in us will be finished, and it will be done to perfection. There is no situation or circumstance that can overcome hope or should lead us to despair. Being like Jesus will put us into the place and position for the greatest opportunities to show His power and manifest His Love to a world that needs to see and know Him. It is a mandate by God that is held up by Scripture that we do what Jesus did during His time in the flesh on earth (John 14:12; 2 Corinthians 5:20).

Hope is revealed through us as we reflect the love of God in all we say and do.

Our faith, love, and hope are manifested in our Christ-likeness as we walk in our predestined paths. These three always remain and are always present. Because of the hope in us, others can know Him as we do. Others can have the same hope that we do. There is no limit to Jesus that would keep Him from being involved in everyone's life. Jesus is not the one who limits the hope we can have; we limit His involvement with us. We think we know everything when we know nothing, because of our limiting Him and the hope that He is.

Hope never fades and never fails; it leads to a true experience of life of growth and victory. This is not an absence of any struggle or temptation but knowledge that we can and will make it through all situations that come our way. We are never without the tests of life, but we are prepared so that we pass through those tests readily. These are opportunities for us to learn, grow, and give God praise and glory.

No matter what we face, we can know and experience God's best.

Hope is never short-changed but is freely shared within our spirits. As faith can do great things in being small (Matthew 17:20), hope too does not need to be large to make a difference. Knowing Him is a process that constantly grows. Hope in any strength is enough to bring us closer to Him. We know Jesus, and that is enough to follow Him. Our relationships are based on Him and what He has done, not on us or what we have done.

He has prepared everything for us to enjoy a full life (2 Corinthians 5:5–8; John 10:10). The stronger our hope, the more powerful our faith, and the greater our love, the clearer the revelation is given of what He has done for us and in us. The closer we stay to hope, the greater the revelation of our victory in Him. With a revelation of Him, our hope is renewed, our faith is strengthened, and our love is released because of what we experience, learn, and do. The more we know Him, the more we can share with others.

The greater our hopes, the greater opportunity for others to know Him and to become like Him.

Our focus on Him allows us better direction and insight to the plans He has for our lives. It is our focus that slips, not our hope. The enemy of our lives wants to distract us from the inheritance we have been granted. The enemy wants us to lose ourselves in his darkness, trying to convince us we are without the love and favor of God. That cannot be further from the truth, but that lie hammers at our hope.

In darkness, we may not comprehend all that God is doing; in this, we operate by sight, not in the faith we are called to walk in. There is little hope for what we see, but our hope is in Him who is not affected by light or darkness (Psalm 139:12). We hold to hope because there is life and energy that helps us to live to our inheritance.

It is in Him, the hope of our lives, that we actually have life (Acts 17:28). We exist because of the hope we have, and it is in Him that all things are fulfilled. Our hope brings our faith to full force. Because we know Him and all that He has given us, we are more likely to step into the fullness of who we are to become. With our hope strong, we can stand in Him as He has called us to do.

When any event of life does not look as we wished or expected, we might look on our own for ways to escape that circumstance. In these times, the thought is for relief, not necessarily direction to get to the place we should be. Many have been conditioned to look for the quick fix rather than for the more permanent and lasting walk. As hard as it may be to wait, there are times when waiting is the better answer.

Troubling times do not mean that things are wrong. Those times that we judge as negative may just give positive results. God uses all things to the greatest benefit to us and to Him (Romans 8:28). We run the risk of missing an incredible blessing when we settle for the quick fix or choose to look for our expectations to be met, rather than accepting what God is doing for us and in us.

A quick fix doesn't always solve the problem; it may only delay the inevitable trouble. Many quick fixes are just a bandage that hides the wound but has nothing to do with the healing of the wound. A quick fix may not give us opportunity to renew our focus on Him.

In hope we see that the better way for us to deal with any situation is to keep our focus on Jesus and rest in Him (Hebrews 12:1–2; Philippians 3:12–14). He always knows what is best for us and all the purposes and destiny of our lives (Isaiah 46:10).

Hope makes the way clear for us to step in faith and receive blessings we have yet to realize. We will choose what is immediate in our confusion of how immeasurable the love of God is toward us (Ephesians 3:14–21; Romans 8:38–39). His love is incredibly large; it is good to be "lost" in the love of God. We will benefit from Him as much as He loves us. Our hope helps us to draw in to His love where we can be safe.

Losing one's hope or even thinking that hope has been lost can be devastating to any individual. The despair and depression is a heavy weight. It can cause a believer to question all he has believed. It can cause a believer to wonder about her salvation. The loneliness and feelings of isolation will shake a person's grip on hope. It is difficult to feel the love of God and to exercise one's faith when it seems that hope is no longer with us. Added to this can be feelings of loss, bringing with it confusion and weakness.

We reach out for help in these times, and what we need is hope. He is everlasting as our hope—we need to know this, and then we will see our way by faith into the blessings He offers. This is more than a matter of not believing our feelings or even "walking by sight." We must learn to know Him as He wants to be known.

No quick fix or temporary boost can lift us to where we need to be like a strong grip on hope can lift us. Hope, together with faith and love, strengthens us to make it through all circumstances. Hope binds our faith and love together. Hope illumines the path that helps all three—faith, hope, and love—work as they should in each of our lives.

Hope is the bridge and connection between faith and love.

There is an understanding in hope that bolsters the things we see by faith and that which we feel in love. Hope helps us experience the reality of God's love as we move in faith. Because of the reality of our hope, we know that we will walk in faith, exploring the reach of the love of God. Hope knows even without seeing (Romans 8:24–26). There is a blessing to believing in Him without seeing all that He is (John 20:29; 2 Corinthians 5:7).

There is no room for any doubt or confusion when we stand in the hope of who He is in our lives. These three—faith, hope, and love—will remain because they are from Him. They are not based on anything of this world; these three are based completely on Him. They invade this world to restore it and all that is in it to its rightful place and image.

Hope is without compromise but holds to the truth of who God is and His desire for us.

In hope we know that all things will be well (Romans 8:28). We know this not by an experience but by a relationship that we have entered into by faith. It is not what we see but who and what we know, because we know the Father. Because we know Him, we can know all things are working for us and not against us (John 8:19; Romans 8:31). The relationship we have with the Father, through faith in Jesus, goes beyond any experience that we could have outside of Him.

Hope brings to our relationships with Him the strengths of His presence needed to get us through life. Hope is an important element and power that makes life work to our benefit and God's glory. We know Him, and we know the Father, so we have hope. We hope, and that brings to life the faith that brings the kingdom to fruition, and love warms and comforts us.

All three—faith, hope, and love—remain and live, guiding and providing for us in each adventure of our lives. Every gift flows out of the strength of the cord of faith, hope, and love. There is nothing that will stand against you when you rely on the strength of this cord. It is not about an emphasis of one over another. All three are related and are best when operating together. This cord is our way of escape, our way of deliverance, no matter what is brought our way.

Love is the greatest, but love brings the three together in perfection (Colossians 3:14). Any one of the three cannot operate to its fullest without the other. All three remain, live, and abide together (1 Corinthians 13:13). There can never be an over-emphasis of faith, hope, and love.

They are all important to the scheme and establishing of the Kingdom of God.

Hope is the light driving any darkness away, so that we can rise up in all the gifts we have been given. Once a gift is given, it will not be taken away (Romans 11:29). Hope is irrevocable.

Jesus, our hope, will always be with us.

The cord of hope, along with the cords of faith and love, brings strength into the heart of any person, no matter the circumstance or mood. When things begin to look dim, hope is what makes the difference. When things are going well, hope keeps us stabilized and looking forward. The effect of circumstances, pain, and the stress of what we are going through can be determined and measured by the level of hope that we have.

We live or die at the level of our hope, whether it is strong or perceivably absent in our lives. Our capacity for hope can be determined by our experiences with love and the activation of our faith. Our hope is reflected through our lives. Hope is important to all that we are or will become. Our relationships with hope will be seen in our handling of life.

Our relationships with the Father is either made or broken in the grasp or release of hope.

Hope illumines our way for salvation to be manifest in us. In hope, we are ready to grasp all the Father provides for our relationships with Him. In hope, we know that He has done all that is possible to make the kingdom and salvation ours (Romans 8:24). Hope is the element of light that shines in and on the kingdom. Hope brings us to the faith by which we can live.

There is no blind leap of faith; our hope is not by sight. Our faith is fulfilled in our active obedience to what we see and hear of the Father. By knowing and trusting the word and promises of God, hope allows us to strengthen our relationships with Him to know that by faith, we can accomplish all things. Our hope is in the knowledge that Jesus will never leave us and that He has given us power and authority to do the things that He did (Mark 16:15–18; Luke 10:19; John 14:12).

Hope is more than wishful thinking.

Hope holds us up when it seems there is nothing stable around us. We are safe with hope, though we may not see. As silent as some have been about hope, we need to be desperate for it to be active in our lives. Hope was not the command of Jesus. It was not the direct topic of His teaching. Nowhere do we find Jesus commanding us to have hope, yet hope is important to every believer. Jesus' every step and action was part of what encourages our hope to reach its potential.

Jesus modeled hope. He encouraged others to hope. He exemplified what hope is and what it could accomplish in a life. He was the light, and there was no darkness in Him (John 1:5). Jesus is the center of all things, and as He surrounds us with His love, we can be assured of His care for us. He will keep us on a sure foundation, because these three remain and abide in life for us. Jesus called us to come to Him (Matthew 11:28).

It is with Him that our hope has its greatest strength. He chose to bring us hope by His lifestyle and not just His words. He knew the importance and so drew us to Him to make our hope shine brighter. He gives us hope by giving us Him.

His sacrifice upon the cross was a part of God's securing our access to hope.

He has shown Himself as the way for us (John 14:6). This is the absolute by which we should live and set our life courses. This is the truth, and there is no room for doubt. Doubt can keep our faith from working, and it will keep us distracted from our hope. Jesus was directing us to keep our relationships with Him clear of any kind of hindrance or distraction. He is to be first (Matthew 6:33) in order for us to live to the full potential of our inheritance from Him.

He is everything for us, beginning to end (Revelation 1:8, 21:6, 22:13). As the Almighty, He sits on the throne and oversees the kingdom. He knows what is needed and what is best for each of us. Though He did not speak of the need or how to have hope, He spoke of knowing Him and drawing close to Him.

Jesus didn't speak of hope as such, because He was and is our hope (1 Timothy 1:1). Jesus called us to faith in Him. He called us to a relationship with Him. We can come before Him in the throne room (Hebrews 4:16) and partake of His incredible grace.

There was no need to call us to hope, because all the works of His grace gave us hope. Calling us to follow and believe in

Him was our call to hope. In Him, we find all we need and all we should ever want.

When we believe in Jesus, we have everything that is needed and that "pertains to life and godliness" (2 Peter 2:2 NASB). Because He is our hope, He is a necessary part of life. Most will do anything to avoid or escape the loss of hope. That same avoidance, if we are not careful, can cause us to make inappropriate decisions that add to the weight of what we carry, instead of making the load light (Matthew 11:29–30).

Jesus is willing to come alongside of us and walk with us, lending us His strength, so that we will know that He has made a way for us (Isaiah 42:16). Here is our hope, in that we know that He is always there and that He will see us through all circumstances. He stays close to let us know of His great love. It is in that knowledge of His love that we know we always are in hope.

In truth, as a believer, we never lose hope because Jesus can never be lost.

That sounds so simple, but it is true. We may not have the feeling, but we know emotions can be deceptive. We do not move by feelings, but we live by faith. In faith, we see all things come to pass. It is in hope that we know all things will come to pass. All things happen in order to boost our hope, strengthen our faith, and envelop us in His love.

The promise is that Jesus will always be with us (Hebrews 13:5). It is not that we are to lower any expectations, but we are to base any expectation on a proper foundation. Everything that we may know or experience is based on who Jesus is and what He has done on our behalf. The events of His life are the revelation of His love, in which we put our faith, and in that knowledge we are built up in hope. It is upon this foundation of Jesus that we are built. On the strong foundation of Jesus, we will be strong and be able to live life to the abundance that He intended.

He is our foundation (1 Corinthians 3:11). Our relationships to Him are not because of what we did but on what He accomplished for us. Hope is based on our knowledge of Him and all that He is and has done for us, not on anything we have done (Titus 3:5). When we are going through any event that troubles us, we tend to base our evaluations of it on ourselves and anything we may or may not have done. We are not the starting point; Jesus is. There is no help in assigning blame. The help is in knowing who our help comes from (Psalm 121:1–3).

Our hope is our help.

We cannot make right decisions based on us or what we may have done right or wrong. We have to base them on who we know as our hope, for He is the only one who is right and will always direct us in truth. As the cornerstone of every believer's life (1 Peter 2:7–8), He is the standard by which our foundation is set and measured.

When we begin our thinking or make decisions on the basis of our own perceived self-importance, we have already begun the turn away from the true goal. We already put our grasp of hope in jeopardy. Life events do not begin with us; they begin in Him. When we begin at the right point, we are more likely to go in the right direction. The beginning point has to be with Jesus, who is our hope, the author of our faith, and the love that holds everything together.

We do not always recognize that He is there; we will not always know what is taking place. But we do know that when we follow Him, He leads us in the right path (Psalm 23), and He makes us hit the right target (Philippians 3:14). In hope, we rest on His promises, knowing He has already done all that is necessary for us to be free.

Hope rests on what we know He can do, because He has promised to be there for us.

We participate in the plans of God through the hope we are given by His promises (2 Peter 1:4). Through this hope, we can prepare ourselves and others for the fulfillment of the promises of God, which are true (2 Corinthians 1:20). Hope isn't about what we see but about holding to what we know in our hearts and spirits.

We know that Jesus was the manifestation of love from God, and nothing can or will ever come between us (John 3:16; Romans 5:8, 8:37–39). There would be no difference between Him and hope. The things that hope can reveal for our lives are those things that Jesus has spoken, exemplified, and given to us. We cannot be separated from Him (Psalm 139). He can find us anywhere, because He can be found everywhere. Knowing and having a sense of the extent of His presence is having a strong grip of hope.

He, our hope, is a constant reminder that the Holy Spirit is with us and will always be there for us. It isn't about what we see but what we believe in the midst of circumstances. Perceptions can be deceptive. Though we may see the way for ourselves, our Father sees all things, past and future, as it is today, so that He is more than able to make the way straight for us. He adds to our knowledge of Him in order to confirm our hope of Him.

In Him, who is our hope, we can more than overcome and win (Romans 8:37). We have been given this hope, so that we would learn to rule and exercise the authority given to us over the things that He has entrusted to us (Revelation 3:21). By knowing Him and having a relationship with Him, we are brought into the kingdom to live as He wants us to live and to experience the inheritance He has given us.

Those who are His are never lost (John 17:12). He enters our lives so that we can have His eternal life flowing through us. We will not be disappointed in Him (Romans 5:5). He gives us His name as a token for hope. All that His name represents and the authority of that name gives us hope that brings us through to faith. Because of Jesus, we are able to overcome.

We stand in His name, and hope rises. In hope, in Him we know that His best is there for us. This is why it is important to keep a grasp of hope—to comprehend all that He offers. The Father proved through Jesus that we can have hope. We know Him, and in Him we have all that we need or could hope for. It is in Him that we have life and light (John 1:4). Jesus paid a great price so that we can know Him. In that relationship, we are given the hope for more in our lives.

The grasp of hope in our lives is in the deeper understanding and acknowledgement of who He is. This is not a matter of knowing facts of Jesus' life but in knowing Him in a real and intimate way. It is not a means of applying our knowledge of Him to the areas we want but in acknowledging Him in all the areas of our lives. He isn't Lord of just what we acknowledge. He is Lord of all of our lives. He is Lord even of those parts that we do not want to surrender to Him.

We are not to know Him with limits of what we care about; we are to know Him how He wants to be known. Hope and the relationship we have with Him should bring into our lives the joy and peace of His presence (Romans 15:13). If Jesus is our hope, then we should pursue all that He is so that we can obtain all that He has for us.

To gain more hope and to know Him better, we must pursue Him. The more we know Him, the more will be revealed of ourselves. That self-awareness will guide us through the things we may need to repent or surrender. The less we are in bondage to self and the more we are yoked to Him (Matthew 11:29–30), the stronger our hope, faith, and love will be. We need to pursue Him in all the ways He opens to us.

It is not in works that we plan and design in which we know Him more. It is the ways He has designed for us that we know Him more. We pursue Him by knowing His Word. The Bible, as His written Word, is the main source of getting to know Him. His Word reveals His heart and mind and gives us a way to draw closer and to have greater hope.

We know Him more through what others may write or speak. It gives us hope when we learn of His ways, in knowing how He worked through and for others. The testimony of others encourages us to hope, knowing that if they made it, we can too (Revelation 12:11). We build one another up in faith, encouraging one another to be more than we are.

The encouragement of each other keeps the hope within us shining bright, keeping Him as the focus in our lives (Ephesians 4:11–13). We will never lose our way when the light is so bright. We can keep one another in this light of hope by sharing our own strength with those who need it. We are a body, the body of Christ (1 Corinthians 12:27). We need to act as such, keeping ourselves in shape in order to endure all things to His glory. We hope together so that none are lost or injured. It isn't about just us but all who believe.

We strengthen our hope by spending time with the Word and each other. The gifts of the Spirit and Holy Spirit, moving freely and on each other's behalf, are important to our capacities for hope. In our pursuit of God, we need the Spirit of God to fill us with His presence, reviving us to keep hope vital. This is to be a constant, filling even to the point of overflowing.

We are never truly filled until we are overflowing.

The Holy Spirit needs to move throughout our lives, helping and strengthening us from within (John 14:26). There are times that we may not have clear discernment of what is taking place, but the Spirit of God within us will pray through us (Romans 8:26–27). This will keep our hope in line with the plans of God. We are led, and we walk by the Spirit (Romans 8:14; Galatians 5:25). Our dependence on the Spirit of God is seen in all we do and the strength of our hope.

The active presence and involvement of the Holy Spirit in our lives is led by a life of prayer and meditation. The open communication between us and the Father will guide us through the Word for the greatest benefit to our lives. Our conversation with Him will help us in our personal walks with Him, giving our hope the knowledge needed to allow us to live by faith.

Remember, prayer involves talking with God and listening to God. Hearing from Him builds our faith because of the hope He shares with us (Romans 10:17). Within these conversations, we are given opportunity to learn from His great wisdom and knowledge. We can meditate on these things to fuel our walks in hope. Meditating on what He gives is the process of allowing His Word to become a part of our everyday lives and existence.

Each individual needs to find those things that help strengthen his or her hope. Our hope is affected by things we listen to or what we read. Whether we listen or read for knowledge or for entertainment, we need to choose for growth and encouragement.

Anything we may choose should have the criteria of being able to reveal to us what we need to rest in our hope. It should reveal more of the image of God in us when we read or listen or even watch. Not everything will have a label of being "Christian" or "spiritual," but we can find energy in it to rise above any circumstance and know we are being cared for and will make it through. That is the power of hope.

Jesus remains faithful to us, as He is all we need for life.

He is our hope, and that gives us light, so then in faith we see and hear all that can happen. He opens the doors and makes the crooked places straight in order for us to walk in His blessing. Hope lifts us to a place where our faith can grasp the purposes of God, no matter the ruin or beauty that surrounds us. Faith and hope are not ruled by our circumstances but in His appearing. He appears as an open revelation of God's love for us. Hope is tangible and very connected to our faith. We are enveloped by His presence and move according to the love and hope He shares with us.

In our knowledge of Him, hope puts the substance to what we see, to what our faith is focused on. Hope fulfills the Father's promise that He will always be there. Through hope, we know that the places that are hard to navigate and the places that are treacherous will be made flat and walk-able. There is a light in hope that dispels any fear and opens the door to our blessings. We do have hope within us.

Jesus is our hope, and He dwells within us (1 Corinthians 6:19). Our hope knows that we will rise above anything that will try to hold us back or destroy us, because there is a mighty presence in us (1 John 4:4). Hope is as enduring as He is. Jesus is from everlasting to everlasting, and that makes our hope as everlasting.

We know Him, and our hope is in Him.

LOVE: THE GOD-POWER

The subject of love should be an easy topic to discuss. Many others from different walks of life have been a part of the discussion and writings on love. There are stories, poems, and songs about love. Some presentations are to provoke more love. Some try to give examples of love. And there are others that express their desire and need for love. There are those that try to teach and define love. There are many different mediums used to express it all. Yet the cry of so many is for love.

The purpose of this writing is to encourage love and to be loved as intended by God; this is to strengthen each one of us to be better. The hope is that we will learn to respond in love, no matter how others respond to us. This isn't about romance or marriage; this is about a life that is full of love in expression and in identity at all times, in all situations, and under all circumstances.

There may not be anything new in this presentation, but it may serve as a reminder of what God has said. He has told us in definite ways that He loves us. This should serve as a reminder to receive love and to love better and more.

We all could get better at love and mature more in love. Growing in something keeps things alive. Learning how love can be manifested best through us takes growth on our part. We learn to open our minds and hearts to the greater world of God and His love. Love needs to be studied and practiced until we get better at it and get it right. We need to know love in more than a casual way.

Love is more than an acquaintance, more than an expression. We need to know love in its essence, persona, manifestation, and all its truth. It is better to know love in its reality than remaking or redefining it to match our reality.

Love will always change our reality for the better.

People tend to pass themselves off as experts on love, but they have no understanding of real love. We all can outline what we feel or want to feel when it comes to love. Each of us has had unique experiences that have influenced our ideas and definitions of love. These experiences have been negative and positive. They will remain with us our entire lives.

Our experiences with love will shape our decisions and choices throughout life. Love is a high priority for our pursuit of life, God, and truth.

The pursuit of love is more than a pursuit of happiness.

Each individual thrives when loved. When we love and feel loved, we feel alive, and things around us are more real. When we love and are loved, something within us inspires and motivates us to live at new capacities. Out of our experiences of love come the poems, goals, music, and so on that make us alive. Through love, we seek new adventures and new experiences and seek to share them with others.

Love makes a difference in our lives and the quality of our lives. Love is more than we can imagine. Love is limitless in its power and blessing (Ephesians 3:19). We need to try to learn how far love can go. We will find that this is an eternal pursuit. We were made for eternal purposes and for eternal life; it is through love that we reach the potential of our destinies.

When love is absent from our lives, we do not grow. We do not have inspiration or motivation. We seek something that we are not sure of. When love is absent, we may try different things, looking for what will fill the gap in our lives. Unfortunately, some of the things we use as a substitute for love have no connection to love, and then they prove harmful to us. There is no real substitute for love—there is never truth in them. Nothing can ever be a substitute for love.

Nothing will do what love can do in our lives.

Love affects many areas of our lives. Sometimes these effects are involuntary, but they can have a very deep impact in our lives. Love is more than an emotion; it isn't as elusive or temporary as that. Love is not as unpredictable as emotions. But it will, at times, draw very strong emotional responses. Love is more than a physical response to someone or something. Yet we know that it does affect us physically at times.

Couples who are attracted to one another will sometimes describe their feelings by the physical response they feel. Some feel heart palpitations, sweaty palms, and dizziness, and more; this they call love. Some describe sexual acts as love; this isn't true. Some acts express one's feelings of love or their emotion. Some are expressions, however, of faulty thinking and feelings. Other sexual acts are expressions of rebellion against God. Love is more than any of this.

Love is a powerful force in our lives.

Our pursuit of love and our thoughts about love can excite us, motivate us, drive us crazy, make us sick, and much more. Many of our responses are based on what we think of love and how committed we are to knowing and experiencing true love. The power of love can free us and bind us to truths that will carry us through life. In love, we should not look for an emotional or physical response but a response in our spirits that confirm our well-being.

Our response of love will be that we will experience more love and a need to give that love. We will also experience an increase in hope and faith. A proper response of love will be everlasting and not fleeting, such as an emotional or physical response will be. Love is much more enduring and long lasting; it goes beyond time and space. This is why Paul calls for us to grasp the far-reaching power of the love God has for us (Ephesians 3:18–19).

We all want to have the force of love in our lives. In our hearts, we know that it is true love we need, no matter what our prior experiences have been with others and their ideas of love. There is a basic desire in all of us to love and be loved. Deep in us is the drive to see fulfilled all that love offers.

There is knowledge in us that love has what we need. We all desire to feel the warmth of love wrapping its power around us, giving us comfort, strength, encouragement, motivation, and value. In our lives, we reach for that place of His presence, where love is the most fulfilling event and experience of our lives. The power and force of love brings us into place of the best life can offer.

When we use the term "force" in describing love, we are talking about the energy and power that love is to our lives. We cannot get through life without love. Love's energy, love's power, is the fuel for our lives. This love is and represents an absolute necessity for the satisfaction and fulfillment of our lives and purposes. Love is more than the feeling and emotion to which so many have reduced it. It is more than a response.

Love is living and growing in us for a purpose higher and bigger than us. Love is our lives.

Life is vital, and love feeds that life. Love makes life larger. We are driven to experience the receiving and giving of love. The drive is to have love as an active part of our lives, each and every day. Love is important to all that we are, each and every day. It is true that we cannot live without love active in our lives.

The drive for love can also present different problems and challenges. It can be our downfall if we are not careful. We can make wrong choices or miss important information for a better decision. The drive for love is so strong that it can contribute to our making wrong choices. We so want to be loved that we will chose almost anything in an attempt to fulfill the longing for love, but it only causes us to feel more emptiness, more dissatisfaction.

Some choices never satisfy but cause our drive to reach uncontrollable levels. We may try different substitutes over and over again, but until we reach true love, there is no satisfaction. True love is revealed in truth, and truth always sets us free (John 8:32). This drive needs to be controlled so that we can best find the love that God freely gives. Discipline gives us better focus to see all that love can be in our lives.

Discipline helps us avoid the mistakes of an overactive drive for love.

There can be times that the drive masks the real need and its best fulfillment. An undisciplined drive may push us into making even more dangerous choices about love and its place in our lives. We may try any substitute, but the effects are unpredictable and are never quite fulfilling. Love requires us to make better and correct choices. Our choices are the guide of our lives; this is an area that is to be covered by God's own love.

His love is always true.

His love will not lead us into anything that will be harmful to us or lead us to do any harm. In His love, there is always openness and truth. There is nothing false in Him. God does not use deceit of any kind, because it never leads to Him or His love. The use of any deceit by God would be a violation of His character; He would no longer be God. If He were to violate His character, then He would not be able to love in the way He should.

His love wants the best for us and out of us.

Love is the best of who He is and what He shares with us. It is out of love that God created us; His love is the foundation of all there is. Because love is foundational, it is of the highest priority to pursue love. We need to experience love in its strength and personality. The more we experience the truth of all that love is, the more we will pursue love. We will want more than just knowledge of love or just a little sampler of love; we pursue the fullness of love's presence to reside wholly in us.

We pursue love so that it so envelops our lives, that it is by love we are recognized.

In the search for love and for the one we love, we can develop expectations. These expectations are not always based on truth.

Many times these expectations are developed out of protection and not out of true need. Due to past choices that caused pain and rejection, expectations develop to keep us from experiencing the same thing again. These expectations are developed to benefit ourselves individually, not necessarily the other person or object of our love.

Any expectation can limit what God may want to do. God, in all His love, can do more than we can expect. We should not limit Him to our imaginations (Isaiah 55:7–9). God sees and knows what the real need is and what can best fulfill that need. Our heavenly Father knows what is best for us, both in the long and short term.

Any expectation is developed to benefit and protect the developer of those expectations. Anyone involved is put into a subservient position to those expectations. There is a control issue when expectations are made. Expectations do not lead to love but will distract from love and all that can lead to love. Expectations do not have a place in relationships. When we list our expectations, we move ourselves out of the realm of love and into an unrealistic realm of further dissatisfaction and frustration. Love does not subjugate another.

Love allows us the place of freedom to enjoy and experience all of God and what He has for us.

The search for love can be a long, exacting, and tiring search. The search for love must be thorough and deep. The search for love isn't just to find it but to find love active in every aspect of our lives. We are in search of the opportunity to release love throughout our lives and to those around us.

This search may be the most important event of our lives, and we must get it right. It isn't about loving the right person but loving him or her correctly. In our freedom, we love as we should. We search for that love and freedom that only comes in knowing the truth. Our decisions about love are based on what we are willing to give and how willing we are to pursue it.

When we grow weary and choose to give up, we may settle for less or some substitute, which never satisfies. If our expectations of love are about what we will get from it, we will be disappointed. If we do not stay alert to all that is happening around us, we can put ourselves into a position to be manipulated into making a wrong choice. Choices are better made with good information, free of expectations and manipulation.

True love only binds us to itself so that we become love.

At some point, the pursuit for love will require us to develop a working idea and definition of what true love really is. We need identifiers to the activities of love in our lives. We need to learn to recognize the working of love in our lives to yield to its way and to follow it better. Recognizing the truth of the love being shown to us will help guide us into further truth and greater love. Limits and controls that we set on our feelings and emotions will help to keep us focused.

We will go to great lengths to feel loved. We define it and its influence on our lives by our feelings. We measure our happiness by our feelings. In much of our lives, we are defined and guided by our feelings and the intensity of our emotions.

Emotions and feelings can be fickle and at times unreliable. Our feelings are not stable foundations. Feelings and emotions can drain us of our energy, causing us difficulties with recognizing love. Love energizes, whereas emotions drain us.

Several things can influence and affect our emotions and feelings. Awareness of these influences can help decipher what we are truly feeling. We make better choices when we have broad understanding of all the influences that call for our attention. These influences do not always take turns but will call all at once, trying to distract us from what we should be concentrating and focusing on. Those influences, at times, are stronger than we originally think. None of them, though, can overcome the power of love.

True love is a stabilizing and empowering force in our lives. This force requires all that we are. The paths of our lives are made straight by love and keeps all things clear. There is no confusion when love is active in our lives. Love makes level the landscape of life so that we can walk as we should in the light of God's love, with confidence and ease.

We may become confused when the voices of life call out to try to keep us from the truth of love. We are never satisfied when confused and distracted. Any confusion and distraction leads us to try to fulfill our needs and desires for love with things that can't satisfy but that draw us deeper into wrong relationships and practices.

The emotionalism of love is not always as healthy as experiencing true love.

Uncontrolled emotionalism can damage us and any relationships we may be working on. There needs to be a guard for our emotions in place to keep us from the harmful relationships and practices that can ruin our lives. This can destroy all that love has worked in us and make it difficult to receive from love what is really necessary in our lives. It is an attack upon us to keep us from the unfailing love of the Father. Love can't be overcome but we can if we are not walking in love.

Love makes us more than we are.

Love is sometimes relegated to a subservient role in our lives, rather than its being the first priority. Something as simple as the food we eat or being hungry can have an effect on how we think and feel. Health issues can lead us into a depression, which in turn can lead to bad decisions. Our physical feelings will cause us to make decisions based on wanting to feel good.

The way we think also influences how we may feel physically. We may cover up pain or other symptoms without changing the root cause of how we feel. This again points to the need of guarding our emotions. It is not always bad, however, that our feelings and emotions have an influence on our decisions. Our feelings are legitimate and point to things that are a part of our lives.

The Bible describes many times where Jesus was "moved by compassion." There are times when a feeling will make us take better notice of what we are doing. An emotion may cause us to recognize subtle points that make us take better notice of what we are doing. This happens when we know ourselves more in depth. This also happens when we know the boundaries and limits of our feelings and emotions. The controls that we set help us to be better, to feel better about ourselves, and show a greater love.

Difficulties can arise when we base decisions on our feelings, which do not always lead us to truth. Something may feel good without its necessarily being good. Our feelings are not always correct. Feelings can be colored by faulty thinking, causing us to misinterpret actions and words. We think we are in love without understanding all that love is or is asking of us.

Love should be the controlling power, not the feelings or emotions.

Love gives us power and the ability to make things right, whereas feelings and emotions usually stir up more feelings and emotions. There is no substance to the cycle of emotions, but love brings unity and perfection (Colossians 3:14).

We need firm foundations built on God's love, with Jesus as the cornerstone (Ephesians 2:20; 2 Timothy 2:19), keeping everything level and in line with His Word. We need to be aware of those who would try to build with slippery or unstable stones of emotion, rather than the firm foundation of love. When our emotions and feelings go all over the chart, it can bring more questions than answers or more instability than direction.

When we battle these instabilities, we can lose focus of our real goal, the eternally strong stability of love. We should not sacrifice true love for the sake of just feeling good. God did not tear the curtain of time and space to walk through the events of the cross just to make us feel good. He did it so that His love would be more available to restore us to His heart and make us as we should be a reflection of Him and His love.

We will not truly feel good until we truly feel loved and can share love. We will feel our best when we have the love in our lives that we desperately need. When we surrender to love, allowing Him to integrate every aspect of our lives, then our foundations are set for us to be good. When love is manifested and when love is operational in our lives, that is when we are at the best of who we are.

Love truly makes the difference to our feelings and emotions. Love is the stabilizing power and force in our lives. It is only in love that we are real. Our true self is exposed by true love. With love as a priority of our lives, we see who we are and find that we are more than we—or others—think.

Love enlarges us to greater capacities of God's presence.

Some choose drugs, alcohol, promiscuous and/or abusive relationships, or eating in order to feel something but confusing it with love. These particular choices have many different causes, but for this writing, we are talking about the effects of love or the absence of it. The strength of our feelings and emotions will have an effect on what we choose and how much we give ourselves over to that choice.

The depth of our commitments to love will determine the ease in which we can move with love in all we do. Those things that move us deeply, that affects us deep in our hearts and souls, that spark our passion, are what we will sell out to. If our hearts are dominated by feelings and emotions, we will be ruled by them (Matthew 6:21). Love will go beyond any limits we may try to establish in order to break through with all its fullness.

Any barrier that can be imagined is incapable of holding back love from reaching our hearts and lives. Love is more than the emotion or feeling that we have for something or someone.

True love seeks what is good and helpful, not just for love but especially for others. Love offers what is healthy, protective, and encouraging.

Love gives of itself in sacrificial ways. Love gives so that others can live and grow. Though we benefit from love, it is really about others feeling the love of God and being blessed through it. You cannot be selfish and have an understanding of love. Love stretches a person beyond his or her perceived limits to points of great outcomes.

One point that may be the most difficult part of love is the giving up of one's expectations and priorities. Things can't always go the way we want them. This isn't about compromising principles or morals but about giving up of ourselves so that others can grow and receive love. This is simple, but not always easy.

Putting others first sounds good but challenges almost everything that has been programmed into us. Societal teaching is about self and all we can get for ourselves. Love is about everyone else. There are those who give an appearance of caring for others, but it is a front to gain attention and influence or avoidance of their own issues. We need discernment to know the difference.

We each may have things that have to be worked through in order to put ourselves into position to truly love and to receive love. Those are minimized when we give ourselves over to love completely, no matter our own feelings or shortcomings. We need to bring ourselves to a place to learn to be comfortable in who we are and what our lives are about. Standing in the purpose and destiny that God has laid out for us gives us greater freedom to know and experience love in its fullness. We should not shortchange ourselves when it comes to love. Being in the right position in God helps keep us focused on Him and His ways.

It is within Him that we find the truth of love. We cannot find ourselves in the right position outside of being in right relationship with Him; there is no love without Him. There is only emptiness when there is no realization of Him in our lives or of His presence around us.

God has done all He needs to do for us to live in the fullness of His promises and grace. He will do even more to make sure we take every opportunity to know Him and to know His love. His acts of love have paved the way for us to come into our inheritance of all that He is and has. Because He has shared of His love for us and to us, we can experience, share in, and give out love as He intended all along.

Love was His motivation to create us.

His love was so large and full, He wanted and needed someone to share it with. His love is why He paid the price and ransomed us through the events of the cross through Pentecost. Because of His love, He did everything to restore our relationships with Him. He missed the times of walking and fellowshipping with us. He will do His all to share His love with us and to have us partake of His love and all that love can open and give for us.

Now is the time that we need to bring ourselves into that position that we can absorb and experience His love to the fullest. As we bring our emotions into control, our lives become steadier. Without the constant shaking of our emotions, we have a better ability to make better decisions. Control does not mean an absence of emotions but having them in their proper place.

The main decision that becomes clearer is the decision to pursue and share true love. Not being encumbered by the out-of-control emotions and feelings that can range from fear to anger and even expectations and anticipations, we can make love a higher priority to experience and share.

In order to control our emotions, we need to learn to put them into the right perspective. We need to know that emotions and feelings are not tangible, so they can change very quickly. There is also a need to recognize whether the emotion or feeling is based on truth; most fears are based on non-realities.

Fear challenges the realities of our thinking.

When we discipline ourselves, we put ourselves in the best position to get all that love has for us as believers. Our thoughts have the Father and His ways as our focus. At any point where the enemy can distract us, fear can enter. These points where fear has entry will be points of the least visibility or feelings of love. Fear is the enemy's greatest weapon. Fear is the web of Satan's lies and deceits.

The enemy will play to our emotions in order to make the most of any fear that he can stir in us. The enemy cannot operate in any other way but in fear. Fear and love are opposing forces. The ultimate defeat of the enemy is the breaking of the power of fear. When we allow love to arise in us, the fear must leave. Love overpowers fear (1 John 4:18). Love keeps us focused on the realities that the Father gives us.

The Kingdom is brought to earth through love.

Love and fear cannot occupy the same space. Our focus and faith will determine which wins. Love will overcome fear unless we make fear the greater focus. Love is always the greater power when we give it a place and freedom to work. The disciplining of our hearts and minds to focus on love does not have to be a painful or stressful practice. Love is empowering, whereas fear drains us of our strength, desires, hopes, and motivations.

Love will allow us to see the best of all that God has to offer for our lives.

Because love always gives the best, it also looks for the best. Love is not a substitute for anything; it is the main and real thing. LOVE is only to be shared and modeled; it cannot be faked. Love is the uniting power of all our emotions.

Our thoughts are influenced by our emotions. But our love should control our emotions. This does not mean eliminating our emotions but keeping our emotions in focus of what truth we are to live in. The truth of God's love is the greatest and strongest reality.

In the truth of love, we can enjoy the greatest emotion and know that we are being cared for and protected. The truth is Jesus and the relationship we have in Him. The truth of love is found in Him and defined by our relationships with Him. We need our emotions to be full but focused. Emotions should not be allowed to flow as a wild river but as a controlled canal. A canal is a directed and focused channel in which all things can flow to the greatest benefit and strength. Life comes through this discipline of channeling the force of love.

The idea and concept of discipline may not connect with the idea of love. When thinking of discipline, the picture that may come to our minds is that of punishment given out. That is far from the truth, especially when dealing with love. Discipline may not be our favorite subject, but it is a necessary practice.

Discipline is the ability to bring into alignment our thoughts, actions, and heart to the path that God has laid out for us. God lays before us the path and makes it straight for us, but we need to discipline ourselves to follow Him and that path (Psalm 37:23; Psalm 119:105; Proverbs 3:6). Discipline leads us away from punishment, but it is not always painless. Discipline brings death to self so that the Father can raise us up in the newness He promised and for us to know Him and His love as He wants us to know Him. As we fade to the background, God increases His presence in our lives. We are enveloped more in His love so that He is seen and not us.

Discipline helps us avoid the wrong steps we may take that lead to harm or punishment. Discipline needs to be strong in order to bring the best results. God isn't looking for ways to punish but for the discipline in our lives so that we can experience the greatest blessing.

There is a "pruning" that can come (John 15:1–7) that takes away the things of our lives that do not produce life and love in us. The "dead and fruitless branches" of our lives can take energy and focus away from where the love and path of the Father are leading us. Discipline is needed so that we are fully focused and energized to take advantage of our full inheritance in Him and His love.

When we discipline ourselves or being disciplined, it is for us to be in line for the greatest manifestation of love. We do not want to miss the mark of the standard of His love. So it is to our benefit to discipline ourselves or to allow the Holy Spirit to discipline us. We are disciplined so that our strength is from the Lord and what we rely on. We cannot rely on our weakness.

Discipline directs us in the truths of what we are to live and believe. The truth of love demands that we stay disciplined and that we do not lose sight of the great prize that God has set before us. Love is the prize that we will gain when we allow discipline to take its place in our lives.

Love protects us and directs us into the greatest blessings and the inheritance God provides.

We need the discipline in order for love to be in our lives in the most beneficial way for the Kingdom of God. Love is a kingdom power, just as discipline is the power to that love. The Kingdom of God is in power, not just words (1 Thessalonians 1:2–5). We are better at love when we handle our discipline with joy. Discipline heightens the benefits and pleasure of love.

Discipline is about having the most fun by realizing the path of the greatest blessing. Discipline is not boring but leads us to excitement, because in discipline there is a protection and a guide to the best of life. Discipline prepares us to meet the challenges and adventure of our lives.

There are many benefits to love's having an active part of our lives.

Love does much to make our lives full and fulfilling. There is not an easy definition for love. Most definitions are more about symptoms or actions of love. Most of the discussion of love is in terms of feelings and emotions.

We probably describe when we are or are not feeling loved, much easier than telling what love really is. We easily recognize the feelings that love can produce or the lack of feelings we have when not love. But giving a clear definition of love can be elusive. Just as Christianity has been defined by dos and don'ts, love is also defined by symptoms and rules. This list can lower the standard for Christianity and love.

It may prove easier to say what love isn't or what love won't do. It is a start until we can completely give ourselves over to operating in love, no matter whether we reach a clear definition. The definition isn't important as walking and living in love. Yet it is important to know all we can of what God wants operating in our lives at all times.

This is what it seems that Paul did in 1 Corinthians 13. Many point to this chapter to say, "This is what love is." But it actually is more of a list of what we do or do not do when we operate with love. It is more a list of ways to recognize the presence or absence of love. Our real search for love is for the person of God and not an emotion, action, or reaction.

Take time to read 1 Corinthians 13:1–13 from the New American Standard Bible:

> If I speak with the tongues of men and of angels, but do not have love, I have become a noisy gong or a clanging cymbal. If I have *the gift of* prophecy, and know all mysteries and all knowledge; and if I have all faith, so as to remove mountains, but do not have love, I am nothing. And if I give all my possessions to

feed *the poor*, and if I surrender my body to be burned, but do not have love, it profits me nothing. Love is patient, love is kind *and* is not jealous; love does not brag *and* is not arrogant, does not act unbecomingly; it does not seek its own, is not provoked, does not take into account a wrong *suffered*, does not rejoice in unrighteousness, but rejoices with the truth; bears all things, believes all things, hopes all things, endures all things. Love never fails; but if *there are gifts of* prophecy, they will be done away; if *there are* tongues, they will cease; if *there is* knowledge, it will be done away. For we know in part and we prophesy in part; but when the perfect comes, the partial will be done away. When I was a child, I used to speak like a child, think like a child, reason like a child; when I became a man, I did away with childish things. For now we see in a mirror dimly, but then face to face; now I know in part, but then I will know fully just as I also have been fully known. But now faith, hope, love, abide these three; but the greatest of these is love.

Let's see what lessons we can gain from Paul's writings and see if we can find ourselves in a better position to recognize and release love in our lives. By going through his observations of love and what many have accepted as a definition, we should find ourselves closer to understanding love and closer to displaying love as we have been intended.

The more we know love, the better we can live it out in our lives. Paul gives us a great foundation, a beginning point to bring love more in focus. A clearer focus on love will allow for a better direction and purpose of our lives. The destiny of our lives is fulfilled by love, and the best way to see love operate in our life is to know love as best we can.

Each verse gives us a perspective of love that can help to make a life of love. It is important to our lives that we make love a priority at every step. Each step we take opens a broader view and world for love. The more that we know of love, the deeper of a relationship we have with love and the greater our lives will flow in love.

The higher level and capacity of life will be seen by the release of love in and through our lives. It is less of a different view of love and more of a greater understanding of things that hide or detour real love. We will see love more clearly when we know what distracts from it and what is a better symptom and fruit of love.

Most who comment on these verses do so within the context of "gifts of the Spirit." Scripture, however, was originally written without the chapter and verse breakdown. The New Testament was written and sent out as letters to specific people. Each book needs to be seen as a whole, with Scripture giving meaning and interpretation. Each verse has a relationship with other verses.

Scripture gives meaning to Scripture.

This chapter relates to all the topics of the entire letter of 1 Corinthians. All topics of this book are related and influenced by the Holy Spirit and how we move under His direction. The Spirit of the Father gives and produces love in us. When we allow love to be the priority and first influence in our lives, all relationships, acts, and thoughts will align to the purposes of God.

Love is to be a part of all we are and all we do and think. We cannot separate ourselves from love (Romans 8:35–39). The capacity for love is built into our very DNA. The capacity and ability to love is a part of who we are. We were created in the image of God and in Him, we see all that love is or can be.

The more we are exposed to love, the more the image of God can be seen in and through us.

> *If I speak with the tongues of men and of angels,*
> *but do not have love,*
> *I have become a noisy gong or a clanging cymbal.*
> —1 Corinthians 13:1 (NASB)

Love is not about how well we can verbalize. Love is not centered on a language. Love can be communicated in any language and by many actions. This is about more than the spiritual gift of tongues. There are some who do not believe that the gifts are in operation today. So they try to make it about the gift and not love. None of the gifts has stopped, but there are some put the emphasis in the wrong place.

Speaking in tongues has its place and priority for a believer, but it is when everything is wrapped in love that we see all things work as they should (Colossians 3:14). There is a better way for life and that is for love to be manifest in all things. Paul is not eliminating any of the gifts, but he is looking to strengthen them in us by refocusing us to love in the way that God has made us to love.

Our communications must be guided by love. It is possible to say things that may be right and good but at the same time are empty because of the lack of love. It is as though there is just noise—Paul describes it as noisy and clanging; that is, it isn't pleasant or helpful. We would generally react by putting our hands to our ears to shut it out.

Some will subject themselves to the noise out of desperation of maybe receiving something out of the noise. Love changes the tone of any communication; it does not matter what the language may be or whether the language is human, angelic, or divine. Love is a language of its own; spoken from the Father's heart through the Holy Spirit into our lives.

Love is so important to life that we are drawn to things that may identify themselves as love but lack the power of it. It is not the words that are necessarily wrong but the lack of real love. If we would add the love we have been given and the love that has been exampled for us, the words would become powerful and creative. With love, the same words that were just noise earlier change into life. The message itself can change when love is applied to our lives.

> *If I have the gift of prophecy, and know*
> *all mysteries and all knowledge;*
> *and if I have all faith, so as to remove mountains,*
> *but do not have love, I am nothing.*
> —1 Corinthians 13:2 (NASB)

Paul is talking about the spiritual gifts in relationship to love. Again, he is not talking of the elimination of the gifts but in moving and operating in the gifts in a better way. This is not a choice of one over the other but in making the best of what we are given.

Not trying to do our best is to make nothing of all we may try to do. Without love all that we may try to accomplish is nothing in comparison to what it could be. Even if God shares the knowledge with us, it is love that makes the difference and adds value to the knowledge. Knowledge is important. Knowledge can be power and influence.

But knowledge without love is empty and measures to nothing.

You can know the future, and you can know about things that others do not know, yet without love it all becomes meaningless. Love gives the means by which knowledge can be shared for the greatest benefit to everyone. Some things do not need to be shared in order for people to be helped and loved. Some knowledge can bring hurt and confusion if not shared properly— if not shared in love.

Knowledge can bring destruction, whereas love builds up and carries us to better places. Love can use that knowledge but does so to build up everyone that may be involved. It is not the origination of the knowledge that builds, it is the love that releases the knowledge that builds into each of us. Knowledge is not the focus but love.

You can know something about someone that can be used to harm them or help them. If the person has a particular weakness or sin that they can't seem to overcome; you can use that knowledge to keep them in bondage or you can help them to strengthen themselves to overcome it (Hebrews 12:12). Love would demand to help them to live in freedom.

> *And if I give all my possessions to feed the poor,*
> *and if I surrender my body to be burned,*
> *but do not have love, it profits me nothing.*
> —1 Corinthians 13:3 (NASB)

It may be a difficult concept for some that to do a good thing may not be the best thing to do. It is actually possible for something good to be meaningless. Feeding those who are hungry is a good thing, but to do so in a wrong attitude may erase whatever good we do. It isn't a matter of withholding from the poor; it is a matter of having love for them to help them out of their situation.

The resolution of this is not to stop feeding or helping the hungry but to do so with love. Even if we were to be offered up in sacrifice, it is meaningless if we do not do it with love. Whether it is for religious purposes or in martyrdom, in sacrifice, love must be present for there to be any difference or true help.

Love freely gives and is increased by its generosity. Doing things in love profits our souls. We do things in love, not for our benefit but for the pleasure and glory of God. The concept of true love is that all we do in love is for others. It is especially for God and for His glory.

Love is not involved or is not a priority when we do anything for ourselves. Love is measured by what it affords others. Love requires an increase of itself so that others will grow and be blessed. Love is outward looking; it is always looking for ways to benefit others and to worship God in truth.

No one would argue Paul's observations about love and the emptiness and uselessness of life when love is absent. Though we help others and do things that may be considered good, without love something is missing.

All the work, no matter how good, is not fulfilling when we do not operate or release love in all things. When we see the worth of living in love we will pursue it more for our lives and for others.

Love is patient, love is kind and is not jealous;
love does not brag and is not arrogant,
does not act unbecomingly;
it does not seek its own, is not provoked, does
not take into account a wrong suffered,
does not rejoice in unrighteousness,
but rejoices with the truth;
bears all things, believes all things, hopes
all things, endures all things.
—1 Corinthians 13:4–7 (NASB)

We can identify the times and actions that are absent of love.

Paul was very clear in describing that without love in operation, there is nothing of value; there is an emptiness that prevails. We know the results when love is absent.

Love gives time to allow things to work out. It is patient, which is to say that love gives all the time necessary for things to reveal it, whether beneficial or harmful. It does not mean that love never shows anger, but it does so in the proper time and in the appropriate ways.

This is not to say that operating in love makes anyone a pushover or weakling. Love, through patience, forces its way because there is a refusal to do anything inappropriate or for itself. Love is about others, and that takes time to allow things to unwrap.

Love released through a person's life is not a collection of "random acts of kindnesses." Love shows kindness by a lifestyle of usefulness. Jealousy is the opposite of being kind. Operating in jealousy is to put oneself in opposition of what is released through others.

Love wants the best in and for others and will not act in opposition to what love is doing in others. Love doesn't allow harm or wrongdoings but gives of itself so that others do not work under wrong motives. In allowing love to be the priority of our lives, we make ourselves useful so that others gain all the benefits of their inheritance in Christ.

Paul continues to show us what love is by stating that it "does not brag and is not arrogant." Love has no need to over-promote itself, draw attention to itself, or build itself up in any way. There is no need to put others down to build itself up. Love, by its very nature, does not look for things to benefit love but for love to benefit others.

To brag or to think more highly of oneself is to violate love's very nature. Love shows the truth of the Father in how He showed us love through Jesus. Through Jesus and the events of His life, love was given its greatest revelation.

It wasn't about what went wrong in the world but what was made right through the truth of the love of God.

Love is based on the truth of the heart of the Father. Love promotes the truth because there is the freedom that is necessary for life to grow and be rejoiced in (John 8:32). In the truth of the love and Word of God, we have all of heaven available to us for the blessings of all who will receive. God loves us unconditionally, deeply, and passionately. There is nothing we can do that will make Him love us more, and there is nothing we can do that will make Him love us less.

He loves us with all that He is. He gave Himself for us so that we will be free and will have access to all the inheritance we have in heaven. The truth of God is strong and allows us to experience all that the Father has for us. In love we give Him all the praise and glory He is worthy of receiving. We worship Him in spirit and truth (John 4:23–24).

Through the strength of love we can understand why Paul said, that love "bears all things, believes all things, hopes all things, endures all things." Love is a strong force in our lives. Love is teamed with faith and hope.

Love is embracing all that we are and can be.

Love's far-reaching power and influence makes our lives better. Love overcomes any impossibility we may face. Our reliance on and surrender to love accomplishes all that is necessary for life and godliness. In love, we find all that we need for life, for it is strengthened with faith and love.

Love can bear all things. That doesn't mean that love will carry everything that life throws at us, but love can build a roof over us; it covers us. It protects us from all things. In the common church, many try to expose everything in a person's life, especially those things that we would rather have hidden. It is almost as though there is no satisfaction until every sin and mistake is known and the person is humiliated. This is not an act of love.

But love covers all things (1 Peter 4:8). This is not to say that sin is not dealt with, but love overpowers the sin, so that it no longer is an issue. Love leads to repentance and a life that is free of all weights that hold us back. There is faith and hope when love operates in our lives. It is a threefold concept for the best of life.

Love transcends any barrier of time and space to help us fulfill the destiny of our lives. Love is never alone. Love takes all that God has available for us in order to keep us in the right paths and focused on Him. Love clears away all that may try to hinder us from living the life we are called to. All of those things that would try to hold us back from our inheritance are made powerless.

Love that has faith sees all things and has the hope to make it through all things.

With love in our lives, we can endure all that life may bring; we can persevere. We can never be overcome when love is in our lives. Our reliance on God and His love allows us strength and power to walk above the things of life and be side by side with Him.

With God in our lives, all things become possible (Philippians 4:13). We are never alone in our pursuit of God and all He has for us. His love dwelling in us carries us through all that life can bring our way. Love "bears all things, believes all things, hopes all things, endures all things."

> *Love never fails;*
> *but if there are gifts of prophecy, they will be done away;*
> *if there are tongues, they will cease;*
> *if there is knowledge, it will be done away.*
> *For we know in part and we prophesy in part;*
> *but when the perfect comes, the partial will be done away.*
> —1 Corinthians 13:8–10 (NASB)

We do not like to admit failure but neither do we easily accept that there is anything in life that doesn't fail. Unfortunately, we have to readily accept failure as a part of life. It is hard to conceive that anyone can rise above failure; even God. By His very nature, God cannot fail (Zephaniah 3:5). But to make us more comfortable with any failure in our lives, we have to reduce God to a lesser role and attribute failure to Him.

Some can make excuses for their own failures and shortcomings because they believe that God has failed with them. But this doesn't make sense to the definition of God. It may bring temporary comfort to blame someone else, but it is only when we take personal responsibility that we have any right of being lifted above failure.

According to Paul, there are things that can fail, even though they are from God. There will come a time when they will become obsolete, though I disagree with some who say that day is now. We need these gifts of the Holy Spirit now more than ever. We are in need of divine help and knowledge during uncertain times. We need these gifts until He comes again.

He is the only one that is perfect, and He is the only one who can fill the gap of our knowledge. Only in perfect love can we see the answers that we need for life. The incoming of the perfection of God does away with the gap of our knowledge. God does not look to handicap us in any way but to complete the work within us (Philippians 1:6). Our Father looks to us in love.

Through love, God fills us, in order to make us complete in Him where there is no failure.

Love is of the heart of God and is a part of His nature. We pursue love in our lives, and that pursuit is a longing for God. Love is what and who God is (1 John 4:8). Everything that God does and thinks is out of a heart of love. Neither God nor love can fail; they will not fail.

They cannot lower themselves or their standards, though they will reach to the lowest depths of life to help and save us. Love will always be there for us. Love can never be done away with and will not be overcome. Love is always victorious (1 John 4:18). Love makes us complete in Him and will always see us through.

When I was a child,
I used to speak like a child, think like
a child, reason like a child;
when I became a man, I did away with childish things.
—1 Corinthians 13:11 (NASB)

There are those who yearn to be young again. They believe there is something better in being young, but that is not the case, especially as we deal with love. As a child, we tend to think of everything for ourselves; whereas love is about everyone else.

We can stay youthful, but we need to mature, not necessarily grow old. There is a difference between being young at heart and being childish. Paul talks about putting away childishness, not about putting away youthfulness. He knows we would be better off looking to be youthful and wise so that love can be released through us in its fullest.

As a child, we give complete trust and affection to anyone who will give us attention and show kindness to us. It is the nearest that many come to feeling love; because a child has not been bent or prejudiced in any way. A child will give his love freely, no matter the look, smell, or style of the person.

Children give of themselves out of the joy of giving, with the thought of receiving something for them. A child is trained to expect something in return, which gives the bend to their ability and capacity for love. Love causes no harm, but the lack and perversion of it will cause great harm. It is no longer love when it is altered or changed.

As children, we enter and enjoy the Kingdom of God (Mark 10:15). With the same energy and excitement of a child, we walk out love in our lives. There is no harm or pain in the Kingdom of Heaven. As we mature in the love of God, we learn to rely on and trust in Him. Childish ways do not allow for growth; the learning process is hampered by the simplicity of the mind, which, in turn, keeps us from the moving in love as we should.

Love moves through hearts that are pure and unbent, just as a child is without the distortions of the experience of deceptions, but is also mature without the childish missteps. Love guards us against being childish but helps us be as a child in faith, always trusting in the Father. We are persuaded to stand in Him.

> *For now we see in a mirror dimly, but then face to face;*
> *now I know in part,*
> *but then I will know fully just as I*
> *also have been fully known.*
> —1 Corinthians 13:12 (NASB)

Love changes our worldview. Love changes how we see life. When we try to view things through our own understanding and with our own concepts, things are not as clear as they could be. It takes love to have a clear view. Love allows us to see without compromise or prejudice.

At most, we only see what affects us. We do not always see life as clearly as we need to, even with the best intentions or understanding. It is though we are looking at a mirror that is made of polished and beaten metal—we see all the hammer marks and the impurities of the metal. The image reflected is unclear, without details.

Our need of God is exposed through our inability to see everything. We need love to help us see Him as He really is. It is then that we can recognize Him in others and in the working of life. Partial vision limits our surrender to Him and the fullness of His love.

We look in a mirror to see ourselves as we are, but it is just a reflection. A reflection is not a true representation of who or what we are. There will come a time when we will be face-to-face with Him, just as they were in the garden. At that moment of being face-to-face with Him, we will know all that we need to know about Him and ourselves. We will see our real image as we were first created. There will be no shame or embarrassment because we are finally seeing Him.

It is in His face, we see who we are, because it was in His image we were created. In seeing Him, we will know Him as He wants to be known. There is no veil or distortion between us, and it is in that exposure that we learn about Him and about ourselves. Just as all the fullness of God dwelled in Christ (Colossians 2:9), in looking at Him, we will know all that we need to know. Love is never in hiding, but we at times hide from love. Love wants to be known completely.

Love freely gives of itself.
But now faith, hope, love, abide these three;
but the greatest of these is love.
—1 Corinthians 13:13 (NASB)

There are three constants in life—and two of them are not "death and taxes." Of all that we may go through in life, both good and bad, of all that may be a part of any of our lives, it is faith, hope, and love that will live on and that are foundational to our lives. These three help us walk and live in the faith, hope, and love that God has provided for us, so that we walk in the fullness of His blessing and our inheritance. These are what dwell for us, bringing us into the life God had intended from the very beginning. This is our greatest pursuit: love.

In this pursuit, we have all that He has provided. We especially have Him. We pursue what we can have and what we can share. Love is fortified and is exposed by our faith and hope. God doesn't ask anything of us that He is not willing to provide the means and ways to accomplish. He will not set us up for failure in any way. He has given of Himself so that we can be all that He created us to be. He loves us with all He is and so He wants that love to have its greatest expression in us.

We can be more than we can imagine because of His work and creative powers in us. In these three—faith, hope, and love— we have all that is necessary for us to enjoy God's blessing and to glorify Him. Love brings it all together for unity and perfection (Colossians 3:14). All the purposes of God are fulfilled in Him because of this foundation of faith, hope, and love He has built in us from the time of creation and reinstated at our salvation.

Love goes beyond any limit or boundary we may set around us. Many limit love by not seeing all that love can be. When a person has any narrow expectations, love is shortchanged in its works and influence—because of love's very nature, our limits are honored. At any moment that we let down our expectations, love will rush in with all power and set things in motion that will lead us to an encounter with God.

The problems we may go through are more than a problem of the lack of love. It is lack of trust and freedom in what love can do and accomplish in us. There is no lack in the Kingdom of God. It would be to everyone's advantage if we would surrender and rely on love. It may not be easy to seek help, but we probably would not be in the situation we find ourselves in if we could do everything on our own. We need love.

Love is the best place of dwelling for all of us; in love, we will have all that is necessary for our lives with Him. He is investing in our destinies and wants to see our purposes fulfilled. All the purposes of God are better served and made clearer when we dwell where He has built for us. We are at our best when we dwell in what remains; faith, hope, and love. Love is the greatest of those things that remain. There is nothing as big or as strong as love.

Love can withstand anything that can try to distract us from God.

The Father wants our full attention, and the enemy will make our lack of understanding about love an obstacle in our pursuits of the Father's heart. Any question or doubt about God's love for us puts the attention elsewhere. Doubts and fear can detour us from the road of love if we allow it, but love will be victorious in us.

His love for us is greater, stronger, and more powerful than anything the enemy may form against us (1 John 4:18; Isaiah 54:17). Only in love will we be victorious and overcome in all aspects of our lives. When faith, hope, and love are released in our lives, we can stand in the power of who He is and what He has done for us and is doing in us.

We need to believe (have faith) and know the truth (hope) that love will bring us through. It is only with that which is strongest and is greater than all else that we can rise above any struggle. Every answer is found in our living and trusting in love. Love has the strength and power to guide and protect us through life's adventure.

We are not lost when we have love operating in our lives.

This is one of the purposes of God's sending His Son—to find we who were lost (Luke 19:10). He came in the flesh to show us the true meaning of love, which we unsuccessfully tried to hide ourselves from (Romans 5:8; John 15:13). His love was and is too strong to hide from. We may try to ignore Him and His love, but eventually, love will always break through and manifest itself in our lives. The image of God that has been created in us will be exposed as we surrender ourself to Him.

No matter where we may place our faith, love will always be there with us (Romans 8:37–39; Hebrews 13:5). Love is more than what its fruit may show. There is more strength, power, and status in love than anything else we may think we can rely on. Only love stands throughout the age and remains the same.

Love is more than what we read about in 1 Corinthians 13. This passage gives us direction and a standard by which we can check ourselves to keep us in the flow of love. As in all things, we acknowledge that Jesus is the goal and the high standard to which we strive.

We are being matured into the "measure of Christ" (Ephesians 4:13). It is in Him we have the greatest revelation and manifestation of love. First Corinthians 13 puts some details to what we should know about love. Our measurement of success is the pattern set for us in 1 Corinthians. We see this in operation and manifested through the life of Jesus.

He was here in the flesh to show us love and to show us how to love.

There are those that look for God to punish and cause suffering. Though we may learn from our and others' failures and mistakes, there are more positive means to learn and to receive. Jesus did not come in judgment; He came in love, to show us the way out of darkness (John 3:17; 1 Peter 2:9). When we pattern our lives after His life, we walk in the path of love.

Because we are in Him, the work that He did is counted to our account (Romans 4:21–24, 5:9). His love for us balances all accounts are given our right standing with God because of His love. We could never pay the debt we incurred when darkness and evil reigned in our lives. But He could and did so, because He was love.

Even at this point, we probably point more at a fruit of love than an actual definition, but the hope is that we will be more apt to demonstrate love as it should be and in its fullness by what we now know. Love is not as elusive as some would have us believe. Neither is love subject to imperfection, just because there are those who want to hold on to their imperfection.

Many hold to the concept of being "only human," to having imperfections in order to try to find an excuse for not moving in or releasing love. But there is more to love than the many fruits and manifestations we have so far discussed. Love is limitless, borderless, and bottomless; the adventure is in exploring the height, width, and depth of love (Ephesians 3:17–19).

Love is better understood in the light of the life of Jesus. We know that He was sent because of God's love for us (John 3:16). He gave all that He could, because He tore into our time and lived within our space so that He could die in our place. He did not allow the darkness or evil to dictate His purposes. He chose to love us no matter what we had done. He knew from the beginning it was going to take an incredible act that only love could make happen.

There is love—the ability to give all of ourselves so that others can live and be blessed.

Love is a sacrifice of oneself to benefit others. There is no question to how much to give; love is the true "all or nothing" proposition. With love, there can be no holding back of any part of itself. We either love or we don't. The choice to love is a simple decision but is not always easy to live up to.

Have you ever thought what would have happened if, when Jesus prayed in the garden of Gethsemane for the cup to pass Him, God let Him go another way? Or what would have happened if while on the cross, when the thieves on the crosses beside Him told Him to save Himself, He chose to do so? Would we have the love of God fully demonstrated to us? I am grateful that we do not have to take those questions seriously, because He did choose to demonstrate His love to the fullest so that we may have life and joy to their fullest (John 15:11, 10:10).

He loves without restraint.

We will sometimes restrain ourselves from all that love affords us. Too many will turn their backs to love out of an unreasonable fear or from faulty. It is what we don't take from love, not what love holds back that leaves us wanting the most. Love will fill-in the blanks of what we need.

Love holds out to us all that we could ever want or need for life; it is then up to us to reach out and receive love. Receiving is our biggest difficulty. Though love gives to us of itself freely, we have a tendency to think that there is nothing free in life. So we put unreasonable conditions on ourselves before we will attempt to take what is freely given.

Love does not come to us out of any measure we have achieved or worked for. Love doesn't come to us because some of us are more worthy or needy than others. Love comes to us because that is what love does. Love seeks to give to us all the best of the kingdom.

The concept that love always gives and sacrifices itself in order for others to grow and be blessed should remind us of someone. Every believer should have a sense of familiarity to this person. For the description of love should lead us to God.

This is who He is: "God is love!" (1 John 4:8 NASB). Of all that we could do to show love to others, we must show them God. When we represent God as we should, we show love. We are His representative, and our first act should be an act of love. Everything we do and think should be an act of love, a giving and sacrifice for others. We should be able to share God and His love with ease in knowing who we are and whose we are.

In giving of ourselves, we give of what God has placed in us—love.

We may know about love, but we can also know love.

We have learned to recognize love in many of the signs and manifestations. Our knowledge needs to grow into a relationship. The more we know Him, the stronger the love that flows through us. There cannot be any separation between our knowledge and relationships with God. Neither can there be an overemphasis of one over the other. We must be balanced in all things that are from God in order to exhibit love in the way that pleases Him the most.

We are to know more than about love; we are to know the person of love. That person is our God and Savior; Jesus Christ. The more we know Him, the more we know love. The greater that relationship grows; the greater our love and capacity for love grows. We not only possess love, but we are possessed by love. A believer's life is a life surrendered to God and in giving and showing love in all he or she does.

The infilling and overflow of the Holy Spirit enriches our capacity for love. As the Holy Spirit flows through us, there comes an increase of possibilities and opportunities for us to know Him better as He wants to be known. The manifestation of God by the Holy Spirit gives an exponential increase in our ability, capacity, and expression of all that love can be in our lives. The more we are exposed to love, the more others can be and are blessed.

Love guides us in the path of the greatest manifestation and blessing of God.

The more we yield to love, the more we will understand what Paul said: "The love of Christ controls us" (2 Corinthians 5:14 – 17 NASB). This is powerful and freeing when understood. His love has a work to do in us. Love will always accomplish its work in us; it is our responsibility to make room and yield to that work.

Much of the rebellion in an individual's life is from the battle of control—the idea is that he or she does not want to be enslaved, controlled, or bossed around. This stems from believing a lie in the beginning of man's existence. We were measuring one person's word over another's, and it was really about who loved us most.

In the lack of understanding of what love is, we tend to express ourselves in a manner that increases the tension, which we fight. It may seem a bit controversial, but to give ourselves totally to the rule and reign of God is the best for us. We are being loved into freedom. When we know the truth (John 8:32), we will know freedom. Love is the purest of truth.

Love controls us by its guidance and prompting to follow the right path, to do what is best for us and others. It is not a control that erases our personalities or our will; it enhances and strengthens who we really are. When we are wrapped in love, the restrictions are only that which is right and good. Love leads to perfection.

Love works according to the Holy Spirit. They are one in power and purpose. Love works according to what Christ did. He sees us through love and the work that He accomplished through the events from the cross to Pentecost. The old creature we were no longer exists because of faith in Him.

An act of faith releases an act of love. His love makes us into the creation that He intended from the beginning, so that we will know Him, His power, and His Spirit. We begin to know Him as He wants to be known and in the way we are to know. In love, we learn to know Him by His Holy Spirit.

Yes, we do have a will that allows us to choose what we want, but when we are in the pursuit of all that God wants for our lives, our will should become the pursuit of His will and way. If we are being true to our relationships with God, we will know that God knows what is best for us and will always know what He wants for our lives.

Knowing that God wants the best for us, we can trust Him to lead us in the right paths (Psalm 23; Isaiah 45:2–3). We could make our own decisions, but we want to please God because of the love we share with Him. Love raises us to a quality of life that surpasses anything we can imagine. When we allow our will to be saturated with love, we are strengthened to make the right decisions and to walk in the trust and faith we have been given.

Because God is so willing to give of Himself, to give freely of His love, we are made more than what we see of ourselves. He has filled us with Himself to raise us to the capacity of all that He is, so that we will stand as His children and enjoy our inheritance from Him.

Love is God and is from God. When we wrap our lives with Him, we begin to see and feel the workings of unity and perfection (Colossians 3:14). Our relationships with love change our lives to lives that are God-influenced and God-emanating. In our pursuit of God and His love, His image, as originally created in us, becomes more exposed to the world. The more we become like Him, the more love is released through us and into the world.

Love becomes the priority when we make our relationships with God the priority.

God is love, and that is who we pursue to make our lives into what it was intended. Love is not what we fight; love is who we surrender to. In love, we make it through all that life brings to us.

We count all things as but a moment and opportunity for joy, because of the love of God living in us (James 1:2–3). All things that work in and through us to make us more like Him are doing so because of love and the power of love. Love will always see us through all that we may go through, and love will make the most of us.

In order for us to really love, we must stay close to love. There cannot be any compromise in what love is doing in us or through us. Love is strengthened by our relationships with God. The work that Jesus did in showing the love of God must be fully released in us. Our faith in Him brings the truth of who He is into our lives. We know that our hope is in Him, because we know Him as He wants to be known. He hides nothing from us so that we can know Him and His love.

The disciplines that we bring to our lives to build our faith in Him are the same disciplines that lets love have its way in our lives. Spending time in God's Word, in His presence and the fellowship of believers, helps us expand our capacity for the love that He so freely gives to us.

Of anything in life, love is the most dependable.

Love is a constant for us. It is because love and God are one, and they are for us. God cannot fail or deny His very nature (Lamentations 3:22; 2 Timothy 2:13). With God on our side, who can be against us? (Romans 8:31). God dwells in us by His Holy Spirit (2 Corinthians 6:16), and where God is, there is love.

Love, being of the Kingdom of Heaven, begins to affect everything in us (Matthew 13:33). As love flows in and through us, the Kingdom of God is revealed. All the power and nature of God dwells and is at work in us. This is a never-ending supply of the love and grace of God.

Our hope is that the more we know God and realize His love, the more we will surrender to Him and the greater the effect on the world. Only with love can we make the difference for the world. With love as our guide, we can influence the world to faith. This is the power of God—His love (1 John 3). The work of love in and through our lives is what brings the focus on God.

We know love because we know God. There is no separation between the two. The more we know Him, the more we love. In love, the world comes to the revelation of God and can make the decision of following Him. The more love you pursue, the more love you can give. Our surrender to God is the sacrifice that brings life to those around us (Romans 12:1–5). Allow your faith to break away any hindrance to the love of God.

The truth of God's love will release the greatest blessing for our lives—His love.

FAITH, HOPE, AND LOVE DWELL IN US

It may seem an oversimplification to say that faith, hope, and love are all we need. But when we come to an understanding of what these three are, we have a better understanding of what they can do in our lives.

Most people want a simpler life, and it can be theirs with faith, hope, and love. Just because it seems simple does not necessarily mean it will be easy. Our focus will turn from our needs and wants to what leads us into the answer of all these things—faith, hope, and love, which we find through our relationships with Jesus. Not everyone or everything involved in our surrender to Jesus is happy or content with the change.

This is where the struggle may come; learning to surrender to Him. Many have become accustomed to the evil or darkness being in charge. It isn't always a matter of being happy with that arrangement. Until Jesus showed up and gave us a better way, we did not know better. Until we were shown the light, all we knew was the darkness and that seemed, for that time, normal and right. Until Jesus showed us what we were losing, we had no comprehension on what we had lost. We were weak in our supposed strength.

It is simple but not always easy to allow the control of our lives to transfer from us to God.

With faith, hope, and love, we are strengthened within, so that we can do what is necessary to please Him (Hebrews 11:6; Philippians 4:13). Jesus has provided for us everything that is necessary for "life and godliness" (1 Peter 1:3 NASB). With Him, we are built up in these three to reflect Him in all we are and do. When we walk in these three, we give ourselves to Him, His way, and His kingdom—just as has been prayed, "Your Kingdom come . . . on earth as it is in heaven" (Matthew 6:10 NASB).

In these three we make all things about Jesus and less about us. He becomes larger as we have become fit for His presence. The more we live in these three, the more we become like Him. These three—faith, hope, and love—will do the work in us to establish the Kingdom of God in us and in others.

When we begin to appropriate the faith, hope, and love into our lives, we find an incredible capacity for Him. There is a point where we are stretched a bit further to make more room for Jesus to move in and through us. Our capacity for Him grows as we increase the activity of faith, hope, and love in our lives and in our circumstances. We will never be the same when these three are an active part of our lives. Not only are we given a greater capacity to manifest Him, but all those around us are affected by these three being active in us.

The faith, hope, and love will allow us to represent Him to others, so that they may know Him as He wants to be known.

We become more than what we think and more than what we were, because these three dwell in us by the Holy Spirit. We are consistently reminded that it is not about us but about Him. These three are all about Him and our relationships with Him. We move in faith, hope, and love so that we please Him. He is the priority, not just the blessing we may receive from the relationship we have in and through Him.

Most of our lives have been about us. We have prioritized our lives according to our wants and needs. When these three are restored and rebuilt in us to their most important foundational place, a shift will take place within us and in our lives. We can no longer remain the same once we have allowed faith, hope, and love to have their rightful place in our lives.

There comes a point in life where these three are no longer conversation topics, but we recognize that they are the foundation stones for our lives. When we stand, we stand in Him (Ephesians 6:11–14a). Standing firm in Him will allow us to reach the capacity of our relationships with Him. As believers, we are growing and maturing into the measure of who God is in our lives.

These foundation stones are laid in alignment with the "chief cornerstone," who is Jesus Christ. We are to allow these to hold us up to enable us to become who we are to be in Him. Jesus becomes the priority in our lives when we bring ourselves into correct alignment with all that He has for us. He is there to take care of us and keep us in the right path.

Because we are in alignment with Him, we are no longer slaves to the world or darkness, but are now children of God (Galatians 4:7). We now move in freedom with faith, hope, and love. All measurement and direction is taken from Jesus. We must discipline ourselves to bring ourselves into the alignment with Him in all things. We are called to "follow Him" (1 Peter 2:21–24 NASB). He will make us into who and what we are to be; we must get into the position to follow and receive from Him.

Each of these three is good and powerful but they are at their best when working together. The greatest is love and is what makes all three work in the capacity of no limits. These three will never fail as they keep us close to Him. They are what we rely on to help us keep the goal in sight and to measure up to His standard (Philippians 3:14). They are what help us to be more like Him and to represent Him as He desires. These three make the image of God that is in us more manifest and recognizable.

With faith, hope, and love working and manifesting in our lives, we become more like Him (1 John 3:2). We become a better representative of Jesus and His kingdom as faith, hope, and love take residence and are established in our hearts and lives.

As we have become stronger in Him, we are stronger in our faith, hope, and love.

Through our active participation with these three, we will find ourselves in position to receive from our inheritance that we have in Christ (Acts 20:32; Ephesians 1:9–14). We are more like Him when we operate under these three. We also show more of God and His image within us when those things that are most like Him are the priority of our lives.

We will find the greater dwelling for the Holy Spirit to make His home when the foundation is bigger and stronger. It is within these possibilities that miracles take place, and lives are changed to reflect Him.

We need to encourage within each other with our faith, which is for the God-possible.

Faith brings answers to our prayers and miracles in our lives. Faith brings us into relationship with God. Faith is about our active obedience to what we see and hear the Holy Spirit doing. Any rebellion, doubt, or unbelief will hamper faith. We must take the risk for the opportunity of seeing what God is doing and seeing that we are in right position to receive from Him.

When everyone else says, "It is impossible," that is when faith is the clearest and strongest. Faith takes us into the kingdom of God, where all things are possible to any who believe. It is by faith we please Him and draw closer to Him. We should come into a new mentality in faith. We need to see our lives situations and circumstances not as tests of our faith but as greater opportunities for faith.

Our faith is our active obedience to what we see the Father do and what we hear Him say to do. Without obedience, our faith will lack substance, and without faith, our obedience lacks the power to make a difference. We can only say we have faith when we do what we are shown to do and what we hear to do.

We have a need to hold tightly to our hope, which is the God-perspective.

We do not wish for things; we have hope in Him because we know Him, and we know what He can do. In knowing Him, we trust in Him; there is the hope. We don't have to understand what is going on; we need to trust Him. Knowing and trusting in Him strengthens our grasp of hope.

Our hope is Jesus. He can be seen and known no matter our circumstances or situations. We will never lose hope. Jesus is always available and will always walk with us. We are built up in Him, who is our hope, and receive a greater power through the Holy Spirit in us (Romans 15:13). Our hope is in Him and is

Him. Hope is a solid foundation stone that cannot be moved or destroyed.

Above everything, we must have love, which is the God-power for our lives.

As faith and hope grows in us, it is love that wraps around us to bring unity (Colossians 3:14). Love is the greatest of the three, because love is able to sustain everything by its power. Love covers all things and brings perfection to our lives. Love lifts us all into the reality of the miraculous. Love brings the Holy Spirit into all things.

Love is God.

With God manifesting in our lives, His love is seen in us, and others are drawn to Him. Love makes all the difference and is the difference. All things we may do or experience as believers is powered and directed by love. The enemy cannot penetrate or overcome the work and embrace of love in a believer's life. Love empowers the faith and hope to perform what God intended from the beginning. He wants us to experience Him and His love in freedom and openness, with no limitations or insecurity.

All three are important to the life of every believer. It is important we find ways to build and encourage these in our lives and the lives of those around us. When these three are manifest and active, then we know that God is moving in ways only He can. These three bring restoration of the plan and purposes of God. It will be as it was before, with us walking with Him, hand in hand and talking with Him, face-to-face.

In faith, hope, and love, it will be as though there was never any evil or darkness. These three work to make things right and to cover all things not of God and to reveal all things of God. In order to experience these to their fullest, we must align our lives with Him and believe as He has called us to believe.

We can take advantage of this stage of humanity. The work of Jesus is done, as has been witnessed from the events of the cross through Pentecost (Romans 5:1– 8). It is by His Holy Spirit that the reality of what He has done is worked through our lives (Philippians 1:6). In faith, hope, and love, we are restored to the place of kinship with Jesus, so that we can live according to our inheritance with Him.

In Him, we can live life as He originally intended, in constant fellowship with Him. Our lives as believers are focused with faith, hope, and love to always bring Him pleasure, praise, and glory. As a companion to God, we know what we are to be about with Him.

We operate best as believers when we allow Jesus to operate through us in faith, hope, and love. In these three, we can encourage and build each other up (1 Thessalonians 5:11). We build more faith, hope, and love in each other, so that God is seen as He intended to be seen and so that He will be known as He wants to be known. God refuses to be reduced to our way of thinking, but He has done all to raise us to His ways.

We are not giving of ourselves as much as we are giving of what He did in us. We work in cooperation with these three, so that God gets the most attention, pleasure, and praise. The more that we focus ourselves on Him, the more He will focus on us.

Growing and operating in the faith, hope, and love that has been freely given to us is an everyday opportunity. God asks us to live freely in these three. For these three to be the most prominent and effective in our lives, we must learn to walk as closely to these three as we can. In this, there will be no separation between us and God; there will be no broken relationship.

We walk as we were created to walk—hand in hand with God and speaking face-to-face with Him. Faith, hope, and love pave the way for our new standing in Him. We have a greater capacity for life with faith, hope, and love in full activation and operation in our lives.

In our walk in these three, they will be seen, not us, which means God is seen through us. They are not for occasional use but for everyday living. The miraculous becomes the normal event of a believer's life. Through the acts of our faith, hope, and love, the miraculous is exciting and awesome but not surprising. A believer's walk is a walk in the kingdom, where God is on the constant move and releases His power.

The activities of faith, hope, and love are not random acts that we may do to make ourselves feel better or feel as if we did something good. The activities of these three are acts from the heart of the Father to make us better and to draw us closer to His heart. These activities are for the benefit of others and for the pleasure of God.

Jesus directs us through the Holy Spirit to fulfill the will of God for others' blessing and for His pleasure. The activities of these three are planned, ordained, and anointed by the Holy Spirit. We are at our best and the closest to the heart of God when we are in full participation with the activities of faith, hope and love. An active life living in the Kingdom of God leads to great adventures of incredible possibilities and opportunities.

There is not a complete list of what the activities are or could be. We know that, as in all things, they must be measured by the commandments of Christ and the rule of the Holy Spirit. We know by which Spirit something is ruled by the confession it makes; the Spirit must confess God revealed Him in the flesh (1 John 4:2–3). Only through this confession do we know that the Spirit is aligned with Jesus and that they will lead us in the right path.

The Holy Spirit of God is given to us so that He will guide and lead us in all truth and teach the ways of the kingdom (John 14:16–17, 26). The more we rely and move in the Holy Spirit, the more that faith, hope, and love will be seen operating in us.

As we learn to walk in the Holy Spirit more confidently and with more assurance, the easier it will be to manifest the presence of God in all we are and do. It is possible that some will wonder why they didn't surrender to the principles of the Kingdom of God sooner when they realize the incredible pleasure that the Father receives and, in turn, blesses their lives.

The kingdom principles and power of faith, hope, and love bring into focus our lives of living in the inheritance we have in Jesus and how everything is so much better when we are guided by the Holy Spirit. The greater we yield to the Holy Spirit, the more we are able to do the will of God and live out what faith, hope, and love are working out in our lives. The more we yield, the more He is able to show Himself and establish His Kingdom through us. The more we submit to Him, the more we will experience freedom.

Every step we take is an opportunity for us to show the world the continuing movement of God.

He is moving in the world in all faith, hope, and love. We are given the incredible privilege to be the ones to show the world that has forgotten how to live in the Kingdom of God. Every chance we take to show our faith, hope, and love is the chance to disciple someone in the ways of the kingdom and to see it established more in others.

We are not wishing for better ways or better times. Neither do we expect that everyone will agree with us. We know that these three will turn everything to the Father. To reject what faith, hope, and love offer is to reject Jesus. Rejection will bring the limits and chains of the evil and darkness into those lives that choose to turn from faith, hope, and love. Jesus paid too high a price to let us simply slide back to the days before He came in the flesh. He will do all He can to keep us from rejecting Him. He will give us every opportunity to believe.

When walking in the Holy Spirit, we are not looking for opportunities to pray for others. We are looking for a chance to reveal the Kingdom of God. Praying is not the option; that is the state of our souls and the life blood of our relationships with Jesus (1 Thessalonians 5:17). Through a life of prayer, we establish ourselves in the faith, hope, and love that exposes the image of God that has been created in us. At last, things will be has God intended, and we will live to the fullest and abundance of His heart.

People are not in need of just a prayer but an encounter and relationship with Jesus.

That encounter and relationship only comes through the faith, hope, and love that we are clothed in and operate by. It isn't a matter of meeting others' needs but in filling the gap of their relationship with God. Others' needs and needed life changes are met by our manifesting God through our faith, hope, and love.

As good and wonderful as it is to feed or clothe someone in need or even to heal someone's disease or release him of pain, unless we manifest the faith, hope, and love, it is all for nothing. It will not have the impact that it should. We work harder, then, to add the necessary faith, hope, and love that is needed.

Jesus came so that we could be restored in our relationships to the Father. The healings, miracles, and such were for the purpose of drawing us back to Him. We are not called to operate as a business but as a representative of God. Our faith, hope, and love are for us to present the full package of God and not just what we are comfortable with. Jesus wants us whole, not just saved or healed or delivered from the evil and darkness.

The greater our capacity, the more active we can be with the plans of God.

By faith, we enter into a relationship with Him. He then has chosen to live in us to be more actively involved with us. When He dwells in us, the faith, hope, and love also dwells in us. He gives us the faith in order to restore our relationships with Him. He is hope, and He is love, which now lives in us by the Holy Spirit.

We are never without Him and never without faith, hope, and love. These three dwell in us to bring us back into right relationship with Him, as it was in the beginning, and to bring us into our inheritance with Him. The focus is upon Him and not on us when these three are active in our lives.

Some may find it strange that we must practice faith, hope, and love. We must put them into practice at every moment of life. We become more at ease in our surrender to the Holy Spirit as we stretch ourselves in these three. The more we practice, the more natural to us it will be to move and operate in faith, hope, and love.

Our greater understandings of what these three are leads to our being able to move in them. As we practice and participate with what can be called the "basic believer's foundation," the stronger and more mature we will find ourselves. Through the training, we will find we change to be more like He intended us to be.

The basic believer's foundation is exactly that—those basic things we do for our salvation and relationship with God. There are certain things that should be first and lasting in our lives in order to build us up in Him. Most people would say that prayer and Bible reading are first and foremost on the list. I would add some things to the list that will help apply the right training to our lives.

Disciplines are to identify the areas that need more attention and better training. This training will strengthen us in our faith, hope, and love. With proper discipline, training, and practice, we learn our need for Him, how to surrender more to Him, and how to trust Him for all things. God has chosen to love us into submission and surrender. By love, He disciplines us into the change that we know (hope) pleases Him.

Prayer is more than telling God what we want. It is more than repeating the Lord's Prayer (Matthew 6:9–13). Prayer is not intensified or made any better by our emotions or volume. Prayer is a very intimate time between us and Jesus. In prayer, we are not just telling Him about what we want or what is going on in our lives. He knows all that. In prayer, we develop our relationships that will keep us in the freedom of faith, hope, and love. Prayer is spending time with God.

Prayer is having a loving conversation with our God.

Prayer is a back-and-forth exchange of words, feelings, ideas, and more. When we pray, we are opening revelations between God our Father and ourselves. Our hearts come together through prayer. This communication and His Word builds and makes secure the establishment of the kingdom in and through us. In knowing God, we know the revelation of faith, hope, and love, which is revealed and build into us through prayer.

Bible reading is also important, but again, there is more to it than just reading a book. It is through the Word that we build our faith (Romans 10:17). We shouldn't measure things by how much we read; but how much we hear from God. Whether it is through reading the Bible, reading a book based on the Bible, or hearing from the Holy Spirit, our growth is determined by our obedience to it and not the quality of what we hear or read.

The Word is more than a representation of God and his Kingdom; the Word is the very presence of God (John 1:1–14). We read and listen to His Word in order to keep ourselves strong and to bring a release of the Holy Spirit. We stay in step with the leading and guidance of the Holy Spirit when we know His voice and know His Word. We learn more of faith, hope, and love.

Our foundation involves more than just the prayer and His Word. These are very important, but we can't stop there. The release and understanding of faith, hope, and love require us to do all that we can. Most of what we need to do, according to the faith, hope, and love, can be learned and done by practice and training in the basic believer's foundation.

This foundational stone includes praying and Bible reading, but it also includes times of soaking and meditation. These are times of allowing the Holy Spirit to just rest on us and allowing the Word to take root in our souls.

The foundation also includes knowing who we are in Christ and living that out in our lives. Proper foundations will teach and show us that living out our faith, hope, and love will be seen in our obedience to doing the things that Jesus did (John 14:12). Following Jesus is being like Him. When we do the things to build ourselves up in Christ, things will happen around us.

We are told that signs will follow us (Mark 16:15–18). These signs and wonders are an extension of our faith, hope, and love, which is an extension of God and His great love. The world needs an experience with the love of God. Those who do not believe need to see how God loves us as believers. The blessings of God that are active in our lives will give others a hunger to experience and know God as we do.

Faith, hope, and love work in and through us for the touching and changing a life by a miracle of the Holy Spirit.

Faith, hope, and love will dwell in us and will establish the kingdom of heaven in our lives. As we come into a better understanding of these things, the more likely we will live, think, and act like He wants us to. The more we live by these three, the more He manifests Himself in and through our lives. By allowing these three to show their abiding and indwelling presence in our lives, we have the best advantage to do the things that please Him and to be like Him.

Our purpose is to please God in all we do. There is no better way than to be like Him at every opportunity.

It is in our best interests and to our benefit to live to the fullest of what we know of faith, hope, and love. These are not concepts that are defined by any feeling or emotion. Neither are they defined by how others feel or imagine them to be. They are only defined by God. Each is a part of His nature and personality. This is the image, which has been a part of us since the beginning, that He is now completing to reveal again through us.

These three—faith, hope, and love—will always be what remains.